GOD
ENCOUNTERS

Lisa Fowler

FOREWORD BY DR. JOSHUA FOWLER

GOD
ENCOUNTERS

Moments That Change Everything

*A*dvantage
BOOKS

LISA FOWLER

God Encounters by Lisa Fowler
Copyright © 2025 by Lisa Fowler
All Rights Reserved.
ISBN: 978-1-59755-840-2

Published by: ADVANTAGE BOOKS™
                Saint Johns, FL,
                www.advbookstore.com

All Rights Reserved. This book and parts thereof may not be reproduced in any form, stored in a retrieval system or transmitted in any form by any means (electronic, mechanical, photocopy, recording or otherwise) without prior written permission of the author, except as provided by United States of America copyright law.

Unless otherwise noted, scripture quotations are taken from the NEW KING JAMES VERSION®. Copyright© 1982 by Thomas Nelson, Inc. Used by permission. All rights reserved.

Scriptures quotations taken from the Holy Bible KING JAMES VERSION (KJV), public domain.

Library of Congress Catalog Number: 2025937591

Name:	Fowler, Lisa., Author
Title:	*God Encounters*
	*Lis*a Fowler
	Advantage Books, 2025
Identifiers:	Paperback: 9781597558402
	eBook: 9781597558600

Subjects: Books › Religion: Christian Life - Inspirational

First Printing: July 2025
25 26 27 28 29 30   10 9 8 7 6 5 4 3 2 1

Endorsements

What Lisa Fowler has put together is an encounter book that will be the catalyst for you to have your own God Encounters. She also shares stories of encounters with Yeshua in Israel. It will be the catalyst for you to fall deeper in love with Jesus!"

Sid Roth
It's Supernatural

****

"I am so thankful Lisa Fowler allowed God to use her in writing this book. God Encounters is more than a book—it's a holy invitation. With vulnerability, insight, and deep spiritual hunger, it guides readers into the kind of divine moments that mark us forever. These pages are filled with stories that awaken faith, stir longing, and remind us that one genuine encounter with God can change everything. This is a must-read for anyone hungry for more than religion—anyone desperate for the real, living presence of God."

Real Talk Kim
Pastor of Limitless Church

****

This book is a powerful invitation into deep, life-transforming encounters with the living God. In a time when so many are longing for real answers, real freedom, and real presence, this message will stir your spirit to pursue Him with fresh passion and expectation. Get ready to be awakened, empowered, and forever changed in His glory!

Rebecca Greenwood
Co-founder, Christian Harvest International

Lisa Fowler

Lisa Fowler has written a precious, honest and powerful book on walking out your identity through Christ. It is deeply intimate and will lead you into encounters with God through practical and powerful experiences with the Savior. If you are dry and thirsty for God or just want a fresh encounter with Him, this book will deeply impact your life.

Cindy Jacobs
Generals International

****

You're going to love this book! Lisa Fowler has the gift and ability to skillfully share her supernatural life-changing God encounters with her reader. Lisa has the power to impart fresh inspiration that activates the readers faith to actually move mountains. I have learned that there is no greater way to win the loss and refresh the over comer than to share a personal testimony from our God encounters. The scripture says we overcome the devil by the blood of the lamb and the word of our testimony. I encourage you to buy this book. Read this book then get several copies for your library so you can have fresh material for distribution to your lost and found friends.

Dr. Clarice Fluitt
Pastor Prophet - best selling author, TV personality, life coach, mentor, entrepreneur, motivational speaker, international Christian leader.

****

Lisa Fowler's spiritual autobiography, 'God Encounters' is a wonderful account of her journey from spiritual infancy to the kind of walk with God that is constantly growing and empowers a person to overcome the various trials that life forces on any human being. I believe that her testimony will be a great encouragement to everyone.

Joan Hunter
Best selling author and founder of Joan Hunter Ministries

God Encounters

Have you ever felt far from God or wondered if He even knows you? In Lisa Fowler's book, "God Encounters" your heart will leap for joy as you read God's love made manifest to you in personal encounters. Lisa not only shares her amazing encounters that connected her deeper with the heart of God ,but gives practical ways for the reader to encounter God. She has incorporated scripture and prayers within the chapters to ignite your heart that God loves you and wants YOU to encounter Him everyday! God has a great plan for you and loves you and Lisa's revelation on God encounters will draw you closer.

Dr. Candice Smithyman
Glory Road TV Host, Your Path to Destiny, author, speaker
www.candicesmithyman.com

****

As a child of God, there is no greater pursuit than encountering your Heavenly Father in a way that marks you forever. Psalm 27:8 says, *"When You said, 'Seek My face,' My heart said to You, 'Your face, Lord, I will seek.'"* This is not a polite invitation—it's a vital necessity. Your life flows from His presence.

We live in a world filled with distractions, counterfeit affections, and spiritual numbness. That's why this book, *God Encounters—That Change Everything*, is not just timely—it's essential. If you've felt the pull to go deeper, to return to your first love, or even begin the journey of knowing your Creator, Lisa's words will serve as a powerful guide.

Tammy and I have had the honor of knowing Lisa for several years, and even early on, we recognized there was more behind her kind smile and quiet demeanor. She carries a deep well of revelation, and in this book, that well begins to flow.

Lisa will stir your hunger, challenge your complacency, and reignite your passion for divine encounters that truly do *change everything*. This

Lisa Fowler

isn't just a book—it's a catalyst. A key that can help unlock your next level of intimacy with God.

Keep pressing in, Keep seeking, And wake up into the encounter that will transform your world.

Barry C. Maracle, Founder of Take Charge Ministries
Author of *Wake Up Into Your Dream*

****

"*God Encounters*" is a heartfelt and tender invitation into the nearness of Jesus. With vulnerability, Lisa Fowler shares her personal moments of encounter with Him, that stir a deeper hunger to know Jesus more. Each story reflects the gentle truth that Jesus longs to be close to us—and that there is no safer, sweeter place than in His renewing love and peace. This book will draw you into a deeper hunger to be close to Jesus, and saturate you in His presence.

Ana Werner
Founder of Eagles Network
Seer, Prophet, Author, www.anawerner.org

Table of Contents

ENDORSEMENTS 5

ACKNOWLEDGEMENTS 13

FOREWORD BY DR. JOSHUA FOWLER 15

INTRODUCTION 17

1: EARLY ENCOUNTERS 19
    ENCOUNTERING HOLY SPIRIT 22
    THE FIRST LETTER I WROTE TO GOD 26
    TOO LAZY TO PRAY 28
    ENCOUNTER PRAYER 30

2: GROWTH IS ESSENTIAL 33
    DOVE ENCOUNTER 33
    JESUS ROMANCING ME! 39
    DOING THE WALTZ WITH JESUS! 40
    THANKFUL 42
    GROWING IS EXCITING 46
    ENCOUNTER PRAYER 48

3: SET APART 51
    THE SECRET PLACE 52
    GET READY, GET READY. 53
    SET APART 54
    PROPHETIC WORD 58
    JUST FOR YOU 63
    SET 65

YOU HAVE BEEN SET APART BY GOD FOR GOD!	68
JESUS AT THE CRUCIFIXION!	68
ENCOUNTER PRAYER	71

4: WILDERNESS ... 75

A POEM TO JESUS	80
WRAPPED IN THE ARMS OF JESUS	81
I HEARD HIM SAY	83
WILDERNESS	84
WHERE	84
INTIMACY WITH THE KING	85
LAVISHES	86
DURING EXTREME RELIANCE	87
NOTHING ELSE SATISFIES BUT HIS SPIRIT	87
ENCOUNTER PRAYER	89

5: THE POWER OF THE FREE ... 93

EXPRESSING OUR FREEDOM	94
FOUR ELEMENTS OF BEING FREE	95
ENCOUNTER PRAYER	104

6: HOW TO ENCOUNTER GOD ... 107

HIS FRAGRANCE	107
A VISION OF THE NATIONS	109
THANKSGIVING IS THE KEY	110
THE GLORY CLOUD	111
HE IS A GOD THAT COMFORTS	112
HOW DO WE ENCOUNTER HIM?	116
HAVE YOU HEARD OF HEAVEN'S SOUND ROOM?	117
FIELD OF GLORY VISION	118
ENCOUNTER PRAYER	119

7: JOY IS GOD'S MEDICINE 123
    THE BEST IS YET TO COME! 128
    ENCOUNTER DECREE 129

Lisa Fowler

Acknowledgements

To my handsome husband: Baby, thank you for believing in me and encouraging me to write this book. The day you told me that you believe this book will provoke people to have their own God encounters and that you were proud of me was the day I knew that I could do this. I couldn't have done this without you.

I love you forever, Lisa

****

To my children: You are too young to understand, but I hope you read this one day and know that I'm so proud of you. I love watching you grow and I love seeing the interest you are showing in Jesus. I love how you pray with a pure and sincere heart.

I love you always, Mom

****

To my parents Eben & Val Black: I am so thankful for the foundation that you laid for me. You taught me from a young age to love Jesus and instilled in me to believe in the power of Prayer. Mom, I still clearly remember your words when I was a little girl - "Jesus can do anything"

I love you dad and mom, Lisa

Lisa Fowler

****

To Dad & Mom Fowler: Thank you for giving me the most amazing man. You have raised a mighty man of God and I'm so thankful to call him husband. Im so thankful for your life and the example you set for not only our family but for everyone around you.

I love you, Lisa

Foreword

By Dr. Joshua Fowler

What an honor and privilege it is to write the foreword for *God Encounters*, the powerful new book authored by my best friend and beautiful wife, Lisa Fowler. From the moment the Lord brought her into my life—across continents, in a church in South Africa—I knew she was someone truly extraordinary. Through the years, I've watched in awe as she has passionately pursued the presence of God with unwavering devotion. Yet, after reading *God Encounters*, I find myself even more deeply moved and grateful that the Lord joined us together as husband and wife.

Tears filled my eyes as I journeyed through the pages of this book. With each chapter, I was stirred—provoked, even—to chase after the Lord with fresh hunger. These encounters are not simply stories; they are invitations. They draw you closer. They awaken your spirit. They leave you longing for more of Him.

In my ministry, I've met many leaders and authors. Occasionally, I've been impressed by their work but disappointed to find their character doesn't reflect their message. That is not the case with Lisa Fowler. She lives every word she writes. What you'll read here isn't theory or theology alone—it's the overflow of her life. Lisa walks with God in a way that is marked by wonder, purity, and an unshakable, childlike faith. Her life is her message.

God Encounters will inspire and challenge you. Whether you're a new believer just beginning your journey with Jesus, or a seasoned leader hungry for fresh fire, this book carries something sacred for you. Each page is an opportunity to cry out, "More, Lord!"—and to experience just that.

Never underestimate what one encounter with God can do. It can change the trajectory of your life and unlock destinies for generations to come. This book isn't just meant to be read; it's meant to be lived.

Lisa, thank you. Thank you for pouring your heart, your tears, your faith, and your fire into these pages. I know *God Encounters* will transform lives—for His glory.

With deep love and admiration,

Dr. Joshua Fowler
AwakeTheWorld.org
Author of *The Five Porches – Rediscovering the Fivefold*

Introduction

God encounters is what I want people to experience. Jesus is truly real and very much alive. Too often I see believers walking around as if Jesus was someone who had been crucified and never rose. With sharing part of my journal and some of my personal encounters with Jesus I hope to encourage fellow sons and daughters of the King and to make clear that He is so real, alive and very active in our daily lives. This is not a book about me telling you how and what to do as a believer, it is merely a personal journey of an ordinary woman with extraordinary experiences with Jesus, a woman who is passionate about pursuing the presence of Jesus and the encounters that she has had with Him.

I often see and hear of people who give their lives to Jesus, and then that's that. They never know what to do from there or they don't really know about having a relationship with Jesus. I can tell you, it's an exciting journey to be on. Hopefully you will personally get to know this great God that you just gave your life to or maybe you read this book and for the first time in your life someone tells you that Jesus is alive. Maybe you've been a believer for years but

never had an encounter with the Great I am. Either way, whoever you are and wherever you're from, my prayer is that you get to know the Creator of all things, that you get to experience this Prince of Peace for yourself.

I cannot even begin to explain how important it is to journal. Too often we forget about the amazing moments we have in His presence, our lives tend to become so busy. We lose track of making time for Him and so often we take those special moments for granted. As we write on a simple piece of paper, or our iPhones and iPads, we re-live the encounter. Once it is written down it's there forever and when the tough times come (and yes those times do come) we can read through what we have written and as we read through those special moments with Jesus, we then realize that He is always with us and ever present in our daily lives, and that's the time we then see the scripture Hebrews 13:5 "For He Himself has said, "I will never leave you nor forsake you." transform from just being information in our minds to impartation in our lives. I trust that as you read through my journey thus far that you will become excited about what God has in store for your own life and that you feel encouraged to write those special moments down.

1

Early Encounters

I grew up in a Christian home. I am so thankful for the foundation that my parents set for me from a young age, teaching me about Jesus and the power of prayer. I gave my heart to Jesus at the age of 3. I remember it clearly. I told my mom, "I am ready." I went to my bedroom, closed the door and kneeled at the side of my bed. My hands were clasped together, eyes closed and I started praying. I asked Jesus to come live in my heart and I told Him how much I loved Him. In that same prayer I asked Jesus if I could get baptized in the same river He got baptized in. At that time my family attended a Pentecostal church. My pastor had a great love for Israel. My 3 year old heart grabbed onto that same passion and it never left. I was told by my mother that I was in my bedroom and prayed for 30 minutes. I would think that was pretty long for a three-year-old. From that day on I had Jesus by my side. I remember "taking" Jesus with me wherever I went. I saved a seat for Him at every pretend play movie and every pretend tea party. I remember as a five year old praying for Him to help me find a special ring I lost, and there it was, as if He directed me right to the spot. There was no doubt in my mind. I just knew He could do anything. I'm convinced that child-like faith is the strongest faith there is, it's that unshakable, immovable kind of faith. He was my best friend.

As time went by and I grew older passing through my teenage years, I totally forgot about having a relationship with Him. I was never a rebellious teenager in fact, I always tried to do the right thing. I prayed every night and read my Bible every once in a while. As we all know, that's not merely enough. There was no relationship with Him.

Teenage years passed and the twenty-mark came. I knew there was something my heart was longing for, I didn't know what but I knew something was missing. Over a period of a few weeks, I lost interest in everything that did not have to do with Jesus. I stopped listening to secular music. I didn't want to watch any other movies other than faith based movies. I had no interest in hanging out with the same friends or attending any of their events. I was wondering what was going on with me. One day I realized it was Jesus that I have not given enough of my time. I suddenly had flashbacks of that little girl who was in love with Jesus. I remembered how He was her best friend and that she told Him everything. It was the creator with whom I was longing to spend time. I was hungry for Him. I was yearning for Him. I was longing to be in a church that was different. I wanted a church that was alive in Jesus. One which seeks the deeper things of God. I wanted to find a Holy Spirit driven church that was passionate about pursuing Him. I found myself visiting church after church but something wasn't fitting. Something wasn't satisfying the calling and drawing within.

A good friend of mine walked into the salon I was working at. This lady told me about the church she attended. She persistently kept asking me to come visit one of their services. I thought it would just be another service that I would come out still searching for answers. Then I thought, what if they forced me to go to the altar or asked me to say something over the mic. I was an extremely shy and timid person, a complete introvert. I eventually agreed to attend a service. One day (I think God physically dragged me) I pulled my nerves together and went to one of their Sunday morning services. Have you ever heard the saying, "one bite and you're hooked," well that was exactly what had happened. I had one taste of the Holy Spirit and I was hooked for life. The pastor gave an altar call for anyone who wanted to rededicate their life to the Lord. My eyes were closed and when I opened my eyes I found myself standing in front at the altar sobbing. I rededicated my life to the Lord and from that day on my relationship with the Lord began and my life has never been the same.

My relationship with Jesus had begun at the age of 20. This is when I started journaling the encounters I have had with Him and also some personal prayers.

This is the first encounter I had with the Holy Spirit. The first time I have ever experienced the Holy Spirit.

Lisa Fowler

Encountering Holy Spirit

I was listening to music while alone in the beauty salon, just minding my own business

While worshipping God, the song "I'm Alive" from Celine Dion came on, and it hit me. The words made me feel as if I were flying with the Lord.

I felt like I was living in in those phrases. I was singing out loud to the Lord, meaning each word.

I was crying and felt myself shaking and realized that all this time I was asking

The Father, "please can I just feel You" and boy oh boy it happened.

I felt His presence all over me. I found myself on the floor between a massage table and a wall. Face planted on the floor, shaking and crying in His Presence. Holy Spirit all over me. All of a sudden I felt more alive than ever before. I came out of that encounter and I felt like I could take on the world.

That was the most amazing feeling in the world. No words, no author, no book can justify the feeling of the Presence of God and to actually realize that He truly is very real and alive is the most eye opening feeling in the world. No person can explain how it feels to be wrapped in His Presence. It's just something you have to feel and experience for yourself. When you come out of an encounter with God you feel invincible, it's as if God himself comes down and sends His electric Glory right through your veins. Oh Holy Spirit, You are the sweetest there is. It's like a breath of fresh air. Little did I know, God had much bigger and more exciting moments in store for me. That was just the beginning of getting to know different aspects of Him. Just a taste. As the level of intimacy with Him grows, so the experiences and encounters with Him become more real, more exciting and more life changing. It becomes more intense. I have found that God can only be as close to you as you allow Him to be. I have come to realize that we can only go deeper in with Him if we choose to do so. His Word, in James 4:8 states, "draw near to God and He will draw near to you." God is the ultimate gentleman, a loving God, He will never force you into a relationship. God will never force you to be in a relationship with Him, I have come to know that we have to decide to be in the relationship and it's up to us to decide to become closer and more intimate with Jesus. I know I want to. Do you?

Just like natural babies are first only able to drink milk, we as newbies in the Lord, or should I say newbies in a relationship with the Lord, have to first drink milk. The Bible says that we should desire the pure milk of the Word. Breast Milk contains the essential vitamins to grow strong. The foundation of the believer lies in the milk. Any relationship needs to have a strong foundation in order to last a lifetime. As we start our relationship with the Lord, we need to drink the milk first to ensure that the relationship will be an unshakable, unbreakable, unmovable, everlasting relationship.

So what is the milk in the Spirit? The milk is the truth of Jesus Christ; it's the foundation of who God is. The milk is where the beginning stages of your relationships with the Lord and the beginning stages of your growth in the Spirit takes place. Milk is the pure Word of God. It is like drinking truth, drinking his Word.

Breast milk protects a baby from infections and viruses, it will better equip a baby's body to fight off any ailments, so does the milk of the Word of God better equip us to fight off principalities, when we have a strong foundation in the Word, we are much more equipped to face battles and opposition.

> *1 Peter 2:2 "as newborn babes, desire the pure milk of the word, that you may grow thereby"*

This scripture tells us exactly how important it is to have the milk first, the truth first and then grow in the truth. It is the pure essence of growth.

I felt nothing at the beginning of the evening, I Couldn't even focus on the songs, my mind was wandering off the whole time. I prayed and asked God to speak to me, to let me feel the Holy Spirit, but nothing happened. We had some fast praise songs and then The Worship songs started. My friend prayed and told me that the Lord told her that I was thirsty for Him. All of a sudden the Pastor's wife started singing prophetically. She was singing everything that I was praying for. During that song the Lord spoke to me. Before that night, I felt as if I had lost God a bit, but in the song, she sang these words; "if you feel as if you lost Him don't worry, He will never leave you." Everything that I was praying for, the Lord answered me in every song thereafter. Re-assuring me that He was with me. At that time I had never heard the Lord speak to me as clear as that before. It felt like He was singing directly to me. I cried and cried, I could hardly stand. I never have experienced Him like that before. This was the first time in my life that I heard Him speak to me.

Once again, no words can describe the feeling of hearing God's voice for the first time. It is a breathtaking moment when we hear the voice of the Creator for the first time. It's an amazing experience when God gives you an instant reply. How amazing it is to have that reassurance that He will never ever leave you. Let me tell a difficult secret to swallow. Whenever we feel as if God has left us, it is just the opposite way around. I have found that these are the times that we don't spend enough time with Him. It is us who leaves Him. Jesus won't force the relationship. He can only be as close as we allow Him to be. The more time we spend seeking His face, the more He reveals Himself to us.

Lisa Fowler

The First Letter I Wrote to God

PRAYER: A letter to my Lord

Father I love You, Father I adore You, You are the anchor in my life. I just want to praise You, I just want to praise You. You are my King of Kings, my life, the centre of my universe.

Father I want You to have a maximum impact in my life, I can feel something big is about to happen in my life, I give You control of my life.

Lead me to great things and let Your Holy Spirit guide me to and on the adventure that You have planned for me.

Father I desire to speak in tongues, in Your heavenly language, I want to prophesy, I want to be Your servant.

God I want You to work through me, to use me to reach one more for Jesus. I want to be a strong, confident woman in Christ. I want to be more like Jesus every day.

I want to hear Your voice in everything that I do and everywhere I go. I love You, You are an awesome God and I want to thank You for Your Love, Your Grace and Your Mercy.

Lord I am so hungry for You, I long to know You, I am thirsty for You. I can feel that I have already grown in the Spirit but

I need more and more and more of You, I need to grow more, I need to know You more. Help me to learn and study Your Word more and more. I want to be covered by Your wings and want to soar with You.

I want to be obedient to Your voice. Thank You for who You are and for loving me through my flaws.

As you see, I was longing to know the one who created me, to be with Him and to experience Him. Without me even knowing at those early stages of growing in the Lord, that my deep was crying out to His deep. The desire to know Him and experience Him was so strong. I just wanted more of Him. God desires for us to long for Him. It is for our hearts to want Him. We were created by Him for Him. We were solely created to worship Him. I cannot wait to share with you my encounters with Jesus, but let's enjoy the journey.

There was a time that I first encountered Jesus. How does one describe to someone else, what it is to see or feel Jesus, I mean He can't physically be in front of us. God works in mysterious ways. He gives us dreams and visions. Through them he reveals Himself to us. That is simply how majestic He is. It does physically feel as if we touch Him. Did you know that God has a certain aroma, a distinct smell, and when it suits Him, we will smell Him, touch Him and see Him. Being a Spirit filled believer has these; out- of- this-world amazingly supernatural advantages. The first time I experienced Jesus was so precious to me. This was the first moment I had with Him.

Too Lazy to Pray

My excuse was that I was just too tired. Our pastor preached that Sunday morning and there was an outpouring of the Holy Spirit. My Pastor was praying for all sorts of things and issues in people's lives.

One of the main things he was praying for (in general) was for people who have become lazy in the Spirit. Wow, then I said, Here I am, Lord!

I'm coming back to You. I closed my eyes and God took me in a vision to a huge field about the size of a football field filled with high yellow flowers. Jesus was standing a distance away with a big smile on His face and with His arms wide open. In this vision I ran as fast as I could.

When I got close to Him I jumped right into His arms. He twirled me around and there I was standing for a long time, wrapped in the arms of Jesus.

Just standing there, feeling His arms around me with my head on His chest feeling His heartbeat. That was the first time that I realized that His heart beats for me. Oh my! He has become the lover of my soul. What a special moment with Him.

God Encounters

I remember that morning so clearly. I was out for the rest of the service, sitting in my chair, not able to concentrate one bit on the message that was preached. I was only able to relive what had just happened. I remember not wanting to come out of that vision and not wanting to leave His arms. I felt so safe and secure. Hearing His heartbeat was breathtaking. You know that feeling of your heart racing when you see someone you have a crush on coming closer and closer. It's the kind of heart-beat that feels like it's going to beat out of your chest. That's the kind of feeling I had with my head on His chest. That's the kind of feeling I had every time I thought about that encounter. I would have sat in that chair the whole day if I could.

Do you know that Jesus 'heart beats for you? It's easy for us to tell someone whom we love that our hearts beat for them, whether it's a boyfriend/girlfriend, husband or our kids, but there's no greater love than what Jesus has for us. His heart beats for us and He wants you to come in close, He wants you to feel and hear his heart beat for you.

The journey of the Spirit filled believer is a journey like none other. Nothing can compare to God's amazing adventures. That first moment with Jesus is an absolute priceless moment in any believer's life. Any moment with the Prince of Peace is a life changing experience and it just gets better and better.

Lisa Fowler

Encounter Prayer

Pray this out loud with me:

Lord, help me grow closer to you. Show me how much you love me. Jesus I want to encounter you. I want to have an experience to be able to tell people about you. Amen.

Encounter Notes

God Encounters

Encounter Notes

Lisa Fowler

Encounter Notes

2

Growth is Essential

Dove Encounter

It was my first time in Israel. How I got to Israel for the first time was a miracle. I was planning to go on a tour that my pastor's parents ran. I had no finances for the trip but every time someone asked me if I was going on the tour I would say, "yes I am going by faith." All I had was a suitcase and a heart that longed to be in the Holy Land. For months I prayed that God would make a way for me to be able to go. Two weeks before the tour started I was praying for confirmation that I would be going. Then I had the most amazing encounter with a white dove. While I was at work one day a white dove flew right into the room and sat on the curtain rail and didn't move for at least an hour. I asked God if this was my sign that I would be going to Israel that year and if it was a sign, could I see this dove again. The next day I arrived at work and there that same dove was waiting for me at the water fountain in the garden. I had numerous encounters with that same dove that day. I stepped outside to get something from my car and the dove was sitting on my car. I went inside and later stepped outside again and that same dove sat on the windowsill. I said to God, "God, are you telling me that I'll be going to Israel this year? And if you are, can I see the dove one more time?" I went outside, I looked up and in the sky was a cloud in the form of a dove. I said, "God you know I don't have the money to go to Israel, but I just know you are telling me that I'll be going." 5 minutes later I got a phone call. The phone call went as such: "Good afternoon, do you have a passport? Your ticket to Israel has been paid in full."

That life long dream of getting baptized in the Jordan river came true that year. God made a way for me to be part of a prophetic women's conference in Israel, I was serving as part of the team and my role that year was to be the photographer. The women's conference had a banquet night at the end of the tour. This was a night to get dressed up in a banquet gown. All of the ladies were going to receive their crowns, to demonstrate being God's queen. This is where we go into the throne room to meet with the King. We had a room made up and decorated to look like a throne room. Each lady had a turn to step into the room to have a special moment with God as their King. I was sitting on the floor behind a table, taking the photos of the women as they went into the throne room. Capturing their special moment was very important to me. I was praying and asking God if I too could have a special moment when I stepped into the throne room. So my turn came, I went in and knelt down but it was not what I wanted. I didn't have that big moment. Seeing all the other women having their wonderful moments with the king inside the throne room and nothing for me was absolutely devastating. I went back behind the table and sat on the floor to take the rest of the photos. Capturing all of the other women's special moments. I felt so disappointed and heartbroken, I was so desperate to have a moment with God just like the other women had. The song "This is my desire" was playing and I began to cry. I cried out and told the Lord that I give Him my whole heart. Sitting on the cold floor behind a table, I was crying out to Him, "Jesus, you can have it all." I asked Him if I could please grow spiritually stronger and for it to happen quickly. It was then when I received my special moment. God then answered me in that precious small still voice and told me, *"You are my princess, just wait and see how far I'll take you."* Those few words directly from my King were so fulfilling and meant so much more than what I could ever ask for. I sobbed. We were supposed to be the queen coming to meet our King but God called me His princess and re-assured me that He had big plans for me. *"Princess"* has now become my nickname, the name God calls me when He speaks to me.

As we grow in the Lord we must be careful not to stay on milk stages, sooner or later we need to go onto solid foods. I know of so many family friends who have been church going people for decades, they boast about how long they've been going to church but there has not been any spiritual growth. We can't stay on the same level forever. There has to be more. There is always more. Yes, staying on milk doesn't keep you out of Heaven, but there is so much more to life than just going to church on a Sunday. We need to hunger and thirst for more. The more we hunger, the more we will be filled. The more we grow and the higher we move in the Spirit the more we can do for His Kingdom. The more He reveals Himself to us the more we live in victory. Moving up in the Spirit means going from victim to victor. Exercise in the Spirit ensures strength in the Spirit. The stronger our Faith muscles become the more we can endure. Instead of being floppy, wishy-washy Christians trying to put one foot ahead of the other we start to run this race with strength and confidence, stamina and endurance. We must be sure of the fact that when God is on our side nothing can be against us or have the victory over us. Loneliness, disease, lack or fear can't bring us down. Being a Believer doesn't mean we won't have to go through some tough times in life. In fact, those tough times are exactly what make us stronger. We do need to go through trials and tribulation. Acts: 14:22 "We must through many tribulations enter the kingdom of God." It's not pleasant to hear or read that scripture, but it is worth it. It is worth going through those tough times, we come out stronger.

The more we hunger and thirst for righteousness, the more we will be filled. The more we seek the deeper things of God, the more we find Him. The more we grow, the more we can face the challenges of everyday life.

> *Isaiah 55:8 "For My thoughts are not your thoughts, nor are your ways My ways," says the Lord.*

We so easily get discouraged when we don't get exactly what we want when we want it. God is after all in charge

God Encounters

but we sometimes tend to forget that He knows best. He knows exactly what we need and when we need it. There I was sitting, hoping and praying that I have a moment just like the women had. I wanted it to happen at the same time as them and in the same place as them but that was not God's plan. He had something different and better in store for me. I love the different ways that God plans our moments together. It doesn't have to be the same as everyone else, we are all different with different personalities. God meets you where you are. He orchestrates encounters with you according to where you are in your walk with Him. You are not going to receive the exact same encounter that someone else had with Him. Your moment with God will be the best for where and who you are. Your encounters with God are not going to be the same as what I have with Him or the same as what any of your friends have with Him. Your moment with Him will be specially created just for you, it will be YOUR encounter. God knows who and what type of person you are. He knows everything about you. After all, He is the one who created you. God knows that I am an adventurous person and that I like to be different and do things differently. Why would I have wanted my encounter to be the same as all the other women's moments in the throne room? I wouldn't know, but God knew that I am adventurous; He knew to work differently with me. He knew that I needed to hear from Him in a different place. I love the fact that He speaks to me in different ways and He meets with me in the weirdest moments of time.

God's thoughts are not our thoughts, our ways are not God's ways, meaning our plans are not necessarily God's plans for our lives. His ways are higher than our ways. I promise you, He does know best. As hard as it might be to go through a disappointment in the sense of not receiving what we want or something not happening when we want it to happen, it is all worth it once we look back and see what really happened. We realize that God had much better in mind than what we had in mind. This is why it is so important to lay our own ideas down and ask God for guidance and direction at all times. I have found that it is so much better to ask God for "God ideas" rather than have our own. Easier said than done, I know. I remember how I have gone through what seemed to be disappointments, when I thought that God was not answering me or not giving me what I thought I needed at the time, but as I reflect back, I see and realize that He had better in store.

> *Song of Songs 2:16 "My beloved is mine, and I am his."*

In that time of my life I was stepping into a romancing season with God, not only is He my heavenly Father, but now the lover of my soul. It was the start of a very intimate relationship with Him. Being intimate with God means spending time with Him, soaking in His presence, sapping up everything He has for you, soaking in worship, digging into His Word, being in longer times of prayer. He is yours and you are His. Being intimate with Him means to spend as much time as possible with Him. Just like the feeling you have when you are in love with your spouse and desire to spend as much as time as possible with him/her. This is the first of many times that God has romanced me.

Jesus Romancing Me!

During a church service, God's Presence was falling. Service was all about climbing God's mountain. I actually wish I could draw a picture of what I saw and encountered. Now for me, seeing a mountain or just hearing the word mountain creates an excitement in my Spirit. During worship, God swept me away in a vision. I found myself on top of a mountain. I was dancing with Jesus. I saw Him in a white robe. He had brown wavy hair hanging on his shoulders. I was dressed in white. He was dancing with me and twirling me around on top of the mountain. After dancing with Him, I walked to the edge of the mountain. I was standing and staring into the distance with my arms folded. I felt absolute contentment. Jesus walked up towards me and stood behind me. He covered me with a prayer shawl. He turned me around and held me with a firm grip on my shoulders. He looked me straight in the eyes and said, "I love you princess." As I type this I'm re-living the encounter. It is so precious to me.

It felt like I was floating on the clouds. Spending time like that with Jesus is priceless. Hearing Him tell me to my face how much He loves me. It was just amazing. That's why it is so important to always have a pen and paper near (or iPad). We tend to forget all that God has done for us in the past but when you sit back and read all about it then you can relive it. This was during a woman's conference in Israel. I was part of the worship dance team that ministered during the conference through dance.

Doing the Waltz with Jesus!

I had to do a waltz type of dance for the opening worship dance. I really struggled to perfect the moves during practices. My team was so gracious and patient with me but I knew I wasn't doing a great job. The evening came to perform the dance, I did it (still not perfectly) but I managed to somewhat pull it off. Everyone loved the dance. At the end of the evening people were lying on the floor just soaking in His presence, each having their own moment with God. I was lying on the floor right at the back of the room behind the chairs. God took me in a vision back to the same mountain where I had my first dance with him. He patiently, step by step, taught me how to do the waltz. I can say with excitement and confidence that He must be the best waltz teacher in the world. The other dancers had a good laugh because every time I stopped crying, I would start again, louder and louder. Tears of Joy, I could not contain myself in His presence. I got up from the floor and I could do the waltz.

I can proudly say I now know how to do the waltz.

Being in a relationship with God is the best relationship you can ever be in. It will be the best decision you have ever made in your entire life. God is so faithful; He will never ever leave us. His heart's cry is for us to be intimate with Him. He wants to reveal secrets to you; He wants to whisper in your ear, He wants to give you strategies and new ideas. God longs for you, He longs to be in your life, He longs to hear your voice but He will never ever force you to love Him.

The love between me and my creator, can't be explained. My desire is to provoke you to want it for yourself, you need to experience this kind of love and the best thing is, He is waiting for you. Just pondering on who He is and what He means to me, makes my heart skip a beat, gives me butterflies in my stomach and makes my knees weak. I am so lovesick for Jesus. Sometimes it feels as if I can't breathe. God's breath is the only thing that can sustain me. The love that God has for us is unmeasurable, unshakable and unmovable. We would never be able to fully comprehend the kind of love that He has for us.

I love what Apostle Paul writes in Romans 8:38-39, "For I am persuaded that neither death nor life, nor angels nor principalities nor powers, nor things present nor things to come, nor height nor depth, nor any other created thing, shall be able to separate us from the love of God which is in Christ Jesus our Lord."

This scripture is pretty much self-explanatory and basically sums it all up. There is absolutely nothing in the entire world that can separate you from the love of Christ. Nothing you do or say will ever change God's mind about you. He loves us through our faults. He loves us through our mistakes; through thick and thin, He is there for us. Nothing we do will make Him love us any less. I love the part in this scripture that says, "nor things present nor things to come." God knows our future. He knows our beginning to end and even the things we might do in the future doesn't change the love that He has for you. It doesn't mean we can continue sinning and think it's all good. God hates sin and He wants us to live a righteous life. No, we are not perfect but we should strive to be Holy in His sight.

Thankful

I am so thankful for God's unfailing love. I'm so thankful to Him for transforming my life and changing me from the inside out and making me a better person. As I read the heading of this chapter, "Growth is essential," I realized that being able to thank Him through the highs and the lows is an absolute key factor in growing in Him. We don't always realize how much we've grown in Christ until we look at where we've come from and look at where we are.

Thankfulness is a sign of maturity. We should thank Him in the highs and thank Him in the lows. Psalms 100:4, "enter into His gates with thanksgiving, and into His courts with praise. Be thankful to Him, and bless His name." Now if there is one scripture that gets me excited, it would be this one. We have free access to the King's courts. We can freely come into our heavenly Father's courts. We should be thankful that we don't live under the law anymore, but under the Grace of God. We can be thankful that we don't have to depend on a high priest to go into the presence of God to ask for forgiveness for our sins. We can go ourselves into the inner courts of God. We have free access to God's presence. We should enter His courts. We should enter into His presence with praise and thanksgiving in our hearts. We should always be thankful to God. No matter what we are going through, it takes maturity to be thankful in the tough times but this I know for sure, there is always something to be grateful for. If you feel like you have nothing to be thankful for, one thing is certain, be thankful for your eyesight for you are reading this book.

Philippians 4:6 "Be anxious for nothing, but in everything by prayer and supplication, with thanksgiving, let your request be made known to God."

There is so much in just this one scripture. First of all, be anxious for nothing. Don't worry too much about that tough situation. God has your back and He will never leave you. We tend to stress so much about the things happening in our lives, instead of just putting our faith into action and trusting God in all situations. I know it is hard, it's not easy being positive in a stressful season, but God has made us a promise. He promised to never leave us. Here's the great thing about going through tough times, it's exactly this; we go THROUGH them. This means we come out the other side. We don't stay there. God carries us through and being able to come through something bad, just means you have another testimony of the greatness of who God is. We can then testify about how God brought us through a difficult time. Praise the good Lord that we don't have to be stuck in a tough time forever. It shall pass! Secondly, pray about everything. There is nothing in the world that you can't tell God. He already knows everything, but He wants to hear your voice, He wants you to tell Him everything. Remember, a relationship comes from two sides. So you can tell God anything, pray about everything.

The scripture says, "by prayer and supplication," supplication in the google dictionary means: to petition, plea, request, urge, appeal. It is OK to cry out to God and request something of Him: to plea for a situation, let Him hear your hearts cry, break open in front of Him, be humble, let it go and let God be.

"With thanksgiving let your request be made known to God." Request something of God with thanksgiving, put your faith into action and thank Him in the waiting. Thank Him before the next door opens. Thank Him before the promotion. Thank Him before the increase. Thank Him before the next great business deal. Thank Him for the resurrection of your marriage even while things are tough. Thank Him for a spouse. The doctors say you can never have children, I DARE YOU, thank Him for your baby. (Please email me when the baby is born) I tell you what; you confuse the devil out of His wits when you thank God in the waiting. The enemy won't have a clue what's going on

because he can't see what on earth you are thankful for, but our God is a great and mighty faithful God. There is power in your thanksgiving.

I am so thankful for what God has done in my life so far. If I just sit for a bit and think about the way God has changed me. I can't help but be in awe of how great He truly is. I might have mentioned this before, but I used to be an extremely shy person, and when I say extremely, I mean extremely with an uppercase E. I couldn't even speak out loud within a group of friends, never mind still speaking in public. I was definitely more of a one person friend. After school I tried serving at a restaurant for extra cash. That did not last long. I was more scared than anything else. I gave most of my tables away to the other servers. Which meant I didn't make a lot of tips. I then started my first official job, a receptionist at a beauty salon. That was so hard. I was not a people's person at all and I had to deal with people with all types of personalities all day long. I was a flimsy, timid and shy young lady scared of the world and scared of making a mistake. Looking back now, I actually feel sorry for that young lady behind the reception desk. She didn't really know who she was and had absolutely no confidence. The day came when I had that encounter with the Holy Spirit and my life has never been the same since. That doesn't mean my life flipped totally around. It was and is a process and I am still growing, and will grow till the day this body dies. I can now boldly proclaim that I am no longer that shy and timid girl. I went from not being able to speak in front of friends to standing on a stage in front of a congregation, opening Sunday morning services, leading people in declarations, preaching, praying for people, praying in a corporate environment and praying for the nations. I now know who I am in Christ. My prayer from that day on was to be a strong, confident woman in Christ and I can proudly say that God is transforming me day by day into the woman of God that he has called me to be.

Growing is Exciting

Growing in Christ is exciting. Learning more about who He is and learning more about who I am is the most thrilling adventure. As the journey goes on, you come to realize all these different attributes, qualities and gifts that God has placed in the inside of you, and all you can do is stand back and stand in awe of how Great He is. David writes In Psalms 139:13 *"For You formed my inward parts. You covered me in my mother's womb."*

It might be quite scary to think that there is someone that actually knows EVERYTHING about you. I mean there is just nothing we can hide from God. Have you ever watched the animated movie "inside out"? God literally knows us inside out. He knows everything about our physical appearance and just as much about what goes on in the inside of us. He knows exactly what is going on in your mind and your heart.

> *1 Corinthians 13:11 " When I was a child, I used to speak like a child, think like a child, reason like a*

child; when I became a man, I did away with childish things."

Growing is truly essential, could you imagine staying an infant for the rest of your life? I don't see the point in that. We were born to grow up, and so in the Spirit, there is no point in going on this Journey with Christ if we don't have any interest in growing in Him. We need to leave the light and fluffy stuff at some point in our lives, how about choosing to do so NOW, by deciding to join me in getting into the deeper and more exciting things of God. There is way more than what we think or can imagine.

1 Corinthians 2:9 "eye has not seen, nor ear heard, nor have entered into the heart of man the things which God has prepared for those who love Him"

So there you have it, I didn't thumb suck or make up the fact that He has bigger and greater things in store for us. It is exactly what the Word of God says, it is God breathed and God ordained. There are better things ahead, the best is yet to come. Our mind just can't fathom all the things He has planned for those who love Him .

So….Ready…Steady….Go…..Lets leap into the deeper things of Christ and with doing so, get ready, get ready, get ready; for you are about to experience Him for yourself. Get ready for a collision with your destiny.

Encounter Prayer

Pray this out loud with me:

Jesus, help me to enjoy the growth and not fight against it. Help me go deeper with you. Thank you that nothing can separate me from your love. Amen.

Encounter Notes

_____

_____

_____

_____

_____

_____

_____

_____

_____

_____

_____

_____

_____

Encounter Notes

God Encounters

Lisa Fowler

Encounter Notes

3

Set Apart

Deuteronomy 14:2: You have been set apart as holy to the Lord your God, and He has chosen you from all the nations of the earth to be His special treasure"

Ephesians 1:4: "just as He chose us in Him before the foundation of the world, that we should be holy and without blame before Him in love"

It is so wonderful to know that we have been set apart by God Himself. He has set you apart as Holy, He has chosen YOU to be His special treasure. As we grow in Christ, one of the most amazing things that we come to realize, is that we have been set apart by God for God and for His purpose. We can easily ask the question; Set apart for what or what does it even mean to be set apart. These lyrics from the song "Set apart" from Worship Central (one of my favorite worship songs) briefly outlines the "what for" question.

Lisa Fowler

"SET APART" by Worship Central

In His presence is fullness of everything that we need. It's in His presence that He can refine us, taking things out of our hearts that aren't meant to be there, changing us from Glory to Glory, yes set apart for His Glory, changed for His Glory, refined for His Glory. It is in His presence that he refines us and purifies our heart. When we spend time with God and get saturated in His presence, we find that He is everything we need. In His presence there is fullness of Joy, full portion of peace full of everything you need in that specific time and season of your life. I challenge you - take time out for yourself, put a worship song on, focus on just worshipping Him, just being in His presence, spending time with Him. I promise you, God will show up and you will experience Him, you will experience His tangible Presence and His sweet Holy Spirit.

The Secret Place

Song of Solomon 2:14 "O my dove, in the clefts of the rock, in the secret places of the cliff, let me see your face, let me hear your voice; for your voice is sweet, and your face is lovely."

There is no word in the dictionary that can explain what it feels like to be saturated in His Presence. I get so excited just thinking about it. When I think about Him, something in the inside of me leaps for Joy. Let's get into: the cleft of the rock, the secret place, that place where it's just you and

God, nothing and no one else, that special place in your heart that nothing and no one but God can enter into. God is inviting you to come into His Courts. God says, "Let me see your face, come spend time with me, let me hear your beautiful voice." I know this can be weird for the male gender. Intimacy with God could be awkward for you. Just remember; there is no gender in the Spirit, no male nor female, nor Jew nor Greek. Galatians 3:28 " There is neither Jew nor Greek, there is neither slave nor free there is neither male nor female; for you are all one in Christ Jesus." Male or female, God wants you for Himself. He wants time with you. He wants to show you what He has planned for you. He wants you to be alone with Him. He wants to reveal Himself to you. Being in a secret place with God is like being under His covering. It is a place that no one can come close to. It's a place of comfort and peace. The secret place is a whole new book on its own, I encourage you to read a book about being in the secret place with Him. It will change your life and how you pursue God.

Get Ready. Get Ready.

We are set apart by our Lover for our Lover, for him alone. This is ultimately what He has set us apart for, set apart from the world and unto Himself for Himself and for His glory.

> *Genesis 2:3 (AMP) "And God blessed (spoke good of) the seventh day, set it apart as its own and*

> *hallowed it because on it God rested from all His work which He had created and done"*

"The word hallowed in this context in this verse means set apart for His purpose. The dictionary meaning of hallowed - set apart as sacred Consecrated and Holy.

Now, it's not just the Sabbath that was set apart and consecrated but so God has consecrated and set us apart. We have been set apart for His purpose.

Jeremiah 1:5 a scripture we all know and yes God was speaking to Jeremiah but all scripture now is for all His children. Jeremiah 1:5 AMP. "Before I formed you in the womb I knew and approved of you as my chosen instrument and before you were born I separated and set you apart, consecrating you and I appointed you as a prophet to the nations.

Yes, not all of us are set apart to be a prophet to the nations, but God anointed and appointed each one of us for a different purpose. God didn't say, "Ok I feel like setting Lisa apart today uh and tomorrow I'll do so for Jack and then Julie. No, before we were born he separated us and set us apart for different things in different seasons of our lives.

Set Apart

As I sat one day reflecting on the concept of being set apart, I was talking to God and said, "Okay, Lord, I want to focus on the 'apart 'part of being set apart. Give me something about this 'apart 'thing." It's amazing how we sometimes tell God what we want to focus on without even asking Him what He wants us to focus on.

So God responded, "Ah, ah." I wish you could hear the tone of His voice—it was like a gentle "No, no." Then He said to me, "I have SET you apart. Forget a little about the 'apart ' part, and let's focus on the 'set.'"

I had to quickly repent for wanting to do my own thing without even asking Him first.

So, I studied the word set and was quite blown away. Set is a verb—and a verb is an action word, right? If I can put it to you like this, it's an "alive" word. According to the dictionary, one of the meanings of set is "to put, lay, stand, place, or position (something—in this case, someone) in a specified place."

God set you apart. He didn't just make you apart or hope and pray that you would be apart from the world. He deliberately chose to set you apart. He positioned you to be apart. He placed you apart. He stationed you apart. Even if you think that you are not important, God chose to SET you apart. You are very much equipped and anointed to do what you were set apart to do. Consider the following people who didn't think they were important at all and didn't even know how significant their roles were—but look at how amazing God is. You might think that you are "a nothing," but in God's eyes, you are everything.

Lisa Fowler

Deborah was SET apart to be one famous Judge.

Matthew was a tax collector and didn't even know, he was SET apart to be one of the twelve to take the Gospel to all the earth.

Anna was SET apart to be a prophetess.

Aaron was SET apart to speak on behalf of Moses resulting in the Israelites being set free out of captivity.

Elizabeth thought she was too old but she was SET apart to give birth to the man who would prepare the way of the Lord.

Mary thought she was too young but was SET apart to give birth to the King of the world.

A woman we give absolutely no credit to? **Pharaoh's daughter** without even knowing, was SET apart to save the baby who would one day lead his people out of slavery.

Joshua, SET apart to lead his people into the promised land.

Paul, SET apart to teach the Gospel of Christ to the first-century world.

Esther was SET apart to save her nation.

God Encounters

All these names I've mentioned, are normal people like you and I, yet God had SET them apart to do great things. Believe it or not, you have been set apart!

These people didn't have the faintest idea that God would use them. He used their gifts and their talents to do great things for His Glory. Yes YOU do have hidden talents and gifts inside of you. Don't you dare think you have nothing to offer. God placed something within you that only you can offer the world. Don't think you are just an ordinary person. God has created you to be extraordinary. The exciting part of it all, is searching and finding those hidden treasures within. What fun is receiving a treasure without having a treasure hunt? There's nothing more exciting than having a map that says "x marks the spot." The Word of God, the Bible is our map, let's take it, use it and find those hidden treasures that God has for us. God takes delight in All that He has created and I can assure you, you are no mistake, you are fearfully and wonderfully made. Ephesians 2:10 "For we are God's masterpiece. He has created us anew in Christ Jesus, so we can do the good things he planned for us long ago." I don't know about you, but I get excited when I read this scripture. We are God's very own masterpiece. Believe it or not, your creator gets excited when He thinks about you. God doesn't make mistakes. He only creates masterpieces. In case you forgot what you actually mean to God, let me give you a quick reminder:

Lisa Fowler

Prophetic Word

I am the King of the world, I became flesh to dwell with you on earth to be with you daily.

I am the truth the way and the life, I am the living word. As I walked the streets of Israel, I healed the sick and raised the dead, there is none like me, no person or thing more powerful than I.

The angels sing of my Holiness. I am your redeemer, deliverer and savior, Whatever you need, that I am, for I am the great I AM.

I loved to teach the Will of my Father.

I was innocent yet sentenced to death. They ripped my clothes,

They beat my skin open, spat in my face, I had a crown of thorns embedded in my head, blood dripping from my face. I was nailed to a cross and took a

Spear driven into the side of my body, I was brutally crucified, but for you my child,

Anything, anything to set you free from slavery, anything to prevent you from being crucified. Through all that torture and excruciating pain, I found joy in knowing that you would be set free. My blood would mean your healing, my blood would mean

Your deliverance, my blood would mean your freedom.

But have no fear for I have risen and am alive forever more.

I have sent my Holy Spirit to be your comforter.

I will never leave you.

My child, this is how much you mean to me.

I didn't come for the animals or the plants. I didn't come for anything but YOU!

I came for you. You are mine and I am yours.

Don't ever think that God doesn't love you. You mean the world to Him. Yes we go through bad things and yes bad things happen to good people. The first thing that comes to mind when we go through something really bad is, "Is God punishing me? or why is God allowing this to happen?" or the favorite thing to say, "God doesn't love me," remember the enemy is the father of all lies, and all those statements are lies from the devil.

How do we learn, grow and strengthen if we don't go through trials? I like to tell myself when I go through a difficult time, "Lisa this is training, you will come out taller and stronger." Some things need to be repeated, It's how the human brain works. The more we read over something, the better chance it will stick. So yes I will say it again, just because we go through things, does not mean God doesn't love us or has forgotten about us. Psalm 23:4; "though I walk THROUGH the valley of the shadow of death, I will fear no evil; for You are with me; Your rod and Your staff, they comfort me." God never promised that we wouldn't ever go through trials and tribulations, God said "when you go through these things, I will be there with you and I will be your comforter. I'm going to say this one more time, and I know what you're thinking, "Lisa, you don't know what I'm going through," believe me when I say and that the Word of God says, GOD WILL NEVER EVER LEAVE YOU, He is faithful FOREVER. That was me screaming it out, hopefully you heard me, read it again, just in case it didn't sink in yet. If there has ever been any doubt in your mind and heart, the doubt is now cancelled, rebuked and gone, never ever to return. No more doubt in the wonderful and powerful name of Jesus.

Back to the whole point of this chapter, "set apart." So let's talk about Elizabeth and Zachariah (John the Baptist's parents) and John himself. Let me give you a quick background.

> *Luke 1:5-7 "When Herod was king of Judea, there was a Jewish priest named Zechariah. He was a member of the priestly order of Abijah, and his wife,*

Elizabeth, was also from the priestly line of Aaron. Zechariah and Elizabeth were righteous in God's eyes, careful to obey all of the Lord's commandments and regulation. They had no children because Elizabeth was unable to conceive, and they were both very old"

Here was a woman of God who thought she would never have children, it was impossible, both her and her husband were old and through all the years of marriage, Elizabeth could not conceive and even if she could, her biological clock has long passed the years of having a healthy baby. BUT, when God has set you apart for something great, nothing can keep you back, nothing can stop you. Not only was Elizabeth set apart to give birth to John the Baptist but she had an amazing encounter with God while John was in her womb.

Luke 1:38 Then Mary said, "Behold the maidservant of the Lord! Let it be to me according to your word."

And the angel departed from her. Mary Visits Elizabeth, now Mary arose in those days and went into the hill country with haste, to the city of Judah, and entered the house of Zachariah and greeted Elizabeth. And it happened, when Elizabeth heard the greeting of Mary, that the babe leaped in her womb; and Elizabeth was filled with the Holy Spirit. Then she spoke out with a loud voice and said, "Blessed are you among women, and blessed is the fruit of your womb! But why is this granted to me, that the mother of my Lord should come to me? For indeed, as soon as the voice of your greeting sounded in my ears, the babe leaped in my womb for joy. Blessed is she who believed, for there will be a fulfillment of those things which were told to her from the Lord.

Have you ever read that story and wondered how Elizabeth knew that Mary was carrying the Lord?

Mary was pregnant with Jesus at the time of this greeting, as soon as Elizabeth encountered Mary, She encountered God and was filled with the Holy Spirit, not only did she have this encounter, her baby within her had an encounter with Jesus. Elizabeth's life was forever changed after this encounter, there was no way that she could doubt what had happened to her. One encounter with the Messiah within Mary's womb and Elizabeth was changed.

Elizabeth does conceive, and she gives birth to the person who would prepare the way of Jesus. Zachariah and Elizabeth had a huge part to play in history, God set these two people apart, to bring forth one of the most passionate people to ever walk this earth.

So what about John, what is so special about him? John, as I said, is one of the most passionate people I have ever read about. I wish I could say that I personally met him, but then I wouldn't be alive in this generation. The Word of God Says about John, "He is a voice shouting in the wilderness; prepare the way for the Lord's coming! Clear the road for

Him!" John was living in the wilderness when he received a message from God. He then parted and went from place to place on both sides of the Jordan river. He preached that people should be baptized to show that they had turned to God to receive forgiveness for their sins. Israel is on one side of the Jordan river, Syria and Jordan is on the other. Jewish people or any Israeli for that matter does not go to Syrian or Jordanian land. It is like walking into a death zone, those lands are arch rivals.

But John was set apart to prepare the way of Jesus. John the Baptist was a wild man. His passion for God outweighed any fear of the enemy. God set John apart and nothing was going to stop him. John lived in the wilderness. His clothes were woven from coarse camel hair, he wore a leather belt around his waist and he ate locusts and wild honey for food. Can you imagine living in a desert only surviving on locusts and honey? God had set him apart. Now please don't think you need to live in a desert and live like a caveman in order to be set apart by God, haha. God chose you and set you apart long before the foundations of the earth. Each person is different and God has a pre designed assignments ready

Just For You

Do you get excited thinking about it? I get excited just writing this. To think that our wonderful, all powerful, all supreme God, wants YOU to make a difference. He created you to make a change. He has set you apart to do something great.

Lisa Fowler

While John was baptizing people, he was actually preparing the people for the coming of Jesus. Matthew 3:11, *"I baptize with water those who repent of their sins and turn to God, But someone is coming soon who is greater than I am – so much greater that I'm not worthy even to be his slave and carry his sandals. He will baptize you with the Holy Spirit and with fire."* So John was set apart by God to prepare the way for Jesus. He knew that there was someone coming who is much greater than anyone who has ever walked the earth. That is a pretty big deal to have that kind of job, to prepare the way of the Lord. John was set apart for a much greater assignment.

> *Matthew 3:13, "Then Jesus went from Galilee to the Jordan river to be baptized by John." Wait what? John had to baptize Jesus! wow! "But John tried to talk him out of it. I am the one who needs to be baptized by you, he said, so why are you coming to me? But Jesus said, it should be done, for we must carry out all that God requires. So John agreed to baptize him."*

Can you imagine yourself baptizing Jesus, that must be the greatest honor and privilege of all time. I can't fathom the idea of man baptizing the Son of God, I don't know if I would be more nervous or more excited. It was the Will of God, and it had to happen like that.

What happened when John baptized Jesus?

Matthew 3:16 "When He had been baptized, Jesus came up immediately from the water; and behold, the heavens were opened to Him, and He saw the Spirit of God descending like a dove and alighting upon Him, "This is My beloved Son, in whom I am well pleased."

Can you see what happens when we are obedient to the will of God? Both Jesus and John had to be obedient to the fact that God wanted Jesus to be baptized by John and not the other way around. As soon as they were obedient, the heavens opened, and God spoke. Even the Holy Spirit came in the form of a dove. I tell you my friends, when we know that we know that God has set us apart, and we are obedient to His will, He will open up the Heavens upon our lives. You will see and hear God more than ever before. He will reveal marvelous things to you, and even better, the sweet Holy Spirit will be there with you. John the baptist was set apart to not only prepare the way of the Lord but also to baptize the Lord.

Set

Let's look at the word set. What do you think of when you read the statement "set apart?"

I always pictured it as God setting me one side for a specific task, knowing that there is something that God wants me to do and only me, an assignment that only I can complete, to an extent it is exactly that. However, when God gave me revelation about this, the eyes of my understanding were enlightened, I had a whole new perspective about the whole being set apart thing, that I am excited to share with you.

First let's look at what this word "SET" means, and also what are some synonyms of the word "SET."

The word "set" is a Verb. As we were taught at school, a verb is a doing word. It is an action word. In other words, I like to say a Verb is an 'alive 'word. So the word "set" is an action. The Word "set" is alive. So that means, when He says that He has SET you apart, he actually did physically set you apart. You were set apart before you were in your mothers womb. Which means that while God was putting stars and the galaxy together, he was working His power and setting you apart. That is just how majestic He is, we shouldn't even try to understand His power. God is supernaturally, amazingly, majestically phenomenal. There are not enough words to describe just how amazing He is. The Cambridge dictionary says that the word "SET" means to put something in a particular place or position. This means that God has already positioned you in the position that he wants you to be in. You might not think you are in a position to do something great for God's glory, but know that God has already positioned you before you were born, you just need to realize what is in the inside of you.

As I am writing this, I hear the Lord say, "your Potential has already been Positioned in the core of your Purpose." We often say that we don't have the potential to do something great. We should stop worrying about whether or not we have the potential to do something. Instead, we should seek out our purpose and when we find out the purpose, there your potential will be waiting for you to do that exact thing. Your potential is waiting inside your purpose. Take a step of Faith and step into your purpose, and then your potential will be revealed.

No matter what your purpose is, there your potential will be. Now that I think about it, let me give you an example. A few years ago I didn't think that I had the potential to write a book, but then God prompt me in doing so, I realized that this forms part of my purpose (so I found the purpose), as I took the leap of faith by simply opening up a clean page and saying, "Lord help," I found the potential to walk out the purpose, meaning I found my potential within my purpose. I found the potential as I was walking out the purpose by Faith. I mentioned in the first chapter, this adventure we're on with God is such an exciting one, that there are treasures that are hidden. So this potential in purpose thing is one example of one of those hidden treasures, just look at how creative and exciting God is. There He goes, revealing to us that our potential is inside of our purpose, just like a gift box or should I rather say a treasure chest. Find the chest, open it up and see the treasure. Find the purpose, open it up, dive into that purpose and see your potential inside to accomplish that purpose.

Lisa Fowler

You have been Set Apart by God for God!

The next moment I had with Jesus must be my favorite of them all, to date. For some it would seem unreal, but for me it was as if I was right there.

Jesus at the Crucifixion!

As I was sleeping, I found myself at the crucifixion of Jesus. I have never felt a dream be so real like this one, I can't explain how real this felt. Jesus was already on the cross. I was standing afar (about a football field) and as I walked up to Him on a narrow path, looking right into His eyes (the most beautiful eyes I have ever seen), hundreds of drunk Roman soldiers on the left and right of me, mocking and teasing me, laughing and shouting, "why do you worship Him? Why do you serve a God of no power?." I ignored them and carried on walking toward Him. I then found myself behind Jesus (I have no idea how I got high enough) leaning on His left shoulder, holding him, cuts and bruises everywhere on His skin, My right hand on His forehead, trying my best to comfort Him. I lifted my head and so did He. As He breathed His last breath out, I breathed His last breath in. As I breathed His breath in, I was filled with chills INSIDE my body, literally from head to toe. I don't mean on my skin. I mean INSIDE. I could literally feel it in my bones. After being with Jesus at the cross I walked down to a beach, I stood at the shore line for a while and out of the waves, there appeared like a foam type wave in the shape of a heart, just to show how God loves me. I heard the Lord say, "I did this for you."

When I woke up from that dream, it felt as if I really, really touched Jesus, feeling His skin, no words can describe. I was still feeling that inward gooseflesh for days after. I mean literally days after this encounter I could still feel the same feeling I had in the dream, I felt those chills in my veins. It was as if I felt his very breath. It was as if His very spirit was flowing through my body. I kept that encounter to myself for at least a year, it was so special to me, I didn't want to share it with anyone. Finally God told me that others people need to hear about the encounter.

I hope you understood this encounter. My hope is that somehow you could experience it and re-live it with me. Being so close to Jesus in a dream, makes it feel so real, and it is real, that's how powerful God is. He can reveal Himself to you in any way that He pleases. He reveals Himself to us in all different kinds of ways, not the same with every person. God even has a sense of humor. Don't be surprised if He makes you laugh and reveals Himself to you in the weirdest way that only you would understand. That's how personal He is. Don't think that all moments with Jesus have to happen at the "Holy times." We have become so religious and forget that God moves whenever and however He wants. God is just so awesome. He shows up when He wants to. Most of my times with Him, or even just the times when I feel His anointing all over, are not in a "Holy" moment. It could be while driving the car, or even in the midst of a conversation with a friend. I remember once, just walking in the desert in Israel. We weren't having a time of ministry, a sermon or even a time of worship. I was literally just walking to get from one place to another, and God's presence fell. I felt His anointing so strong and couldn't believe how powerful He was to just show up like that. I just wept and wept, the people must have thought I was crazy but I felt His Presence all over me.

We need to have our hearts open and ready at all times for God to work and move in our lives. We need to give God 24/7 access to our hearts. We must allow Him to do what He does best. To heal, restore and mend a broken heart, to bring new life, new Joy and to bring out the person you never knew existed. Only He can show you the real you, the person who He created you to be. If God needs to do open heart surgery on you, let Him do it, even though it is very painful, I promise you, you can trust Him with your life. I promise you, God only has good things in-store for you, even if you don't think so. He is a good Father, and makes all things work out for the good of those who love Him. Romans 8:28

While I write this, I can already hear some say, "but too many bad things have happened, and where was God through it all? I have asked the same question, so no judgement from this side at all, God where are you?, is the most asked question in mankind. Right now at this very moment of writing these words, I am sitting here crying out for my own desires and direction, crying out to see His mighty Hand that I so love to talk about, to move in my life. I myself need to hold on to the Hope that He has all things in His hands, with that said, again I have another question, are you still standing? Things do go wrong in life, being Set Apart doesn't mean that all things will always go as planned, most times they don't because of our own decisions, but never did He nor will He ever leave me and He won't leave you. Let God do what He does best. I don't think there will be enough pages or ink in the world to print out all that God can do. The Word of God says that "ALL things are possible with God." The word "all," has no ending, all means all. I don't know about you, but I know for sure that God is no man to lie, so If His Word says ALL then you better know, that all means ALL. Please do yourself a favor, and give your Creator a chance, just a chance to pour Himself into you, just let Him do the work, make the choice to keep your heart open for Him to "DO WHAT HE DOES BEST." You never know, He might just sweep you completely off your feet.

Remember…. you HAVE been SET apart!

Encounter Prayer

Pray this out loud with me:

Thank you Lord for setting me apart. Thank you that you have a plan and a purpose for my life. Thank you that you will never leave me. Thank you for placing potential within me to fulfill my purpose. If you could use ordinary people in the Bible I know you can use me too. Amen.

Encounter Notes

God Encounters

Encounter Notes

Lisa Fowler

Encounter Notes

4

Wilderness

Wilderness, the most dreaded word for a Christian to hear. It's not something people want to talk about. I would like to give you a different perspective on this one.

For those of you who don't know what I'm talking about when I say wilderness. It's a time in your life where you feel all alone. It feels as if nothing is working out. There is no one and nothing around you who understands that you feel empty and dry inside. Basically, you feel like a desert from the inside out. You might feel hopeless, like there is no way out.

I have a little secret to share. Would you believe it if I told you that it is actually a really good thing if you find yourself in a desert season in your life. The wilderness is not that bad, and is exactly where you need to be for that moment. I know it sounds unbelievable and you might be thinking I've gone off my rocket, but God's purposes are always greater than what we see.

Lisa Fowler

Generally I am not someone who stresses about things, anyone who knows me would tell you, I am peaceful, cool, calm and collected. I don't stress about things. Something in my life had to happen for me to get to that point though. Something had to happen for me to finally decide if I would live in fear and stress, or live in Peace and Joy. Only I could make that choice. In life, we are the only people who can make a choice to either live in fear, or live in peace. No one can make that choice for you.

There was a time in my life, still in the early stages of my relationship with Jesus, where my family was going through a tough time. I felt broken. I woke up every day with stress and I went to bed every night with stress. It was a rough patch between my parents. I think we all know that any parental issue affects the whole family. It's my opinion that there is no family on earth who are closer than my family. My parents, brother and I were very close and shared everything with each other. There is not a thing that we didn't know about each other. The closer I got to Jesus, the more the enemy fought my parent's marriage. This was the time I had just started a full on passionate relationship with God. Nothing and no one could get me down. I found myself reading all Christian materials I could get my hands on, I worshipped with every song I heard, even if it wasn't a "worship" song, I would make the words work as worship unto Him. The closer I got to Jesus, the more the devil attacked my parent's marriage.

God Encounters

The more I prayed the more they fought. The more I worshipped, the more they partied. One day I had enough, my friend suggested that I anoint my parent's bed. That made the enemy even more mad. I bought a tiny New Testament bible. One night while my parents had a party at our house, shot glasses were flowing and music was pumping, I went to their room and I knelt by their bed, and poured my heart out in Prayer. I anointed the mattress and placed the Bible under the mattress on my mom's side of the bed. My thought was that even though they didn't know, they would be laying their head on the Word of God. I Walked up and down the room, interceding for the situation. The next couple of days, I thought I made a big mistake because finally the bomb burst and my parents were ready for a divorce. If this situation had happened before I started my relationship with the Lord, I would have been absolutely broken. There wouldn't have been anything left of me. No words can describe how broken I would have been if they had gone through with it. It would have felt as if my whole world collapsed like a building coming down with me right at the bottom. That would have happened IF I didn't have Jesus.

I had to make a choice that day, live in fear or live in peace. I chose to take Philippians 4:7 and make it my scripture to live by, and not doubt it for one second. Philippians 4:7 "and the peace of God, which surpasses all understanding, will guard your hearts and minds through Christ Jesus." I can honestly say, taking that scripture and living by it, having

Faith that God is no man to lie, will absolutely change your life forever. It did mine.

I remember that morning as if it was yesterday, the morning that the "separation bomb" exploded. My parents had enough of each other and the fighting didn't stop. Their marriage was at rock bottom. The enemy was mad because he knew he was about to lose this battle, so he gave his last blow and temptation crept in. This is what I did. I walked out to the patio. I stood there and my words were, "God I chose you, no matter what happens in my life. I know that you will look after me, at this moment I refuse to worry about my parents or anything else. I chose to keep my eyes focused on you. For I know you will provide for me. God you've got me and I know you will never leave me. I have nothing else but to believe that Your Word is true. I let go of everything. I place EVERYTHING in your hands, every worry and every fear, and from this day on, I refuse to worry or stress about anything in my life," Amen. Then I stepped back into work.

From that day I hardly stressed or worried about a thing, I completely surrendered to Faith and lived by faith. The sense of release can't be explained, it literally felt like a mountain off my shoulders. I felt light and free no matter what. I didn't have a worry in the world.

I went through some tough situations and seasons and yes, in that moment some fear dropped in. Whatever happens in our lives, we constantly need to remind ourselves that God has us. He is bigger than anything or anyone we might be facing. When I say, I never stressed about anything, that does not mean the devil didn't try to steal my peace and joy. The devil tried to steal my peace many times, and just when stress and worry creeps in I have to quickly remind myself that I have the victory and everything will be just fine.

What happened to my parent's marriage? My mom had an encounter with God through my white dove testimony. ONE encounter changed everything. I am so honored to say, in the very same year, all in one day, all alcohol and cigarettes were thrown away. There was not one party after that, their marriage was completely restored and they are still very happily married serving God together with a passion for each other as well as passionate for Jesus.

What I struggled with in my early 20's was people attacking my character. I am so blessed and highly grateful that God gave me wisdom beyond my age. At that moment I had people attacking my character and maturity and undermining me. They were talking bad behind my back and tarnishing my name. That's a tough one to deal with, I honestly don't think I was strong enough to deal with it on my own. The hardest thing is to sit back and let God defend your name and not take things in your own hands. Thankfully I had and still do have a phenomenal support group. They are always reminding me that God's got this and that He is on my side. I will never forget my mom's words when we went through something tough. "Lisa, don't forget, the highest trees get the most wind." That does not mean people with titles, she just meant that the closer you get to God, the angrier the devil gets. Don't let that ever discourage you, serving and living for Jesus is most worth it. Nothing comes close to walking and living in God's favor.

A Poem to Jesus

Here I stand with arms wide open
Fill me up with more and more
This living water needs to be outpoured
Fill me up Lord.
I surrender to You on my knees
Do with me just as You please
Messiah I am Yours
I am ready to do whatever it takes
To completely die to the flesh
And to just obey

All I want is for people to experience Jesus through me. Writing this poem, I could picture myself literally standing in an open field with arms stretched open, and God pouring into me from Heaven. I wanted His living waters to be poured out of me for people to want Jesus as much as I wanted Him, people need to experience Him and to realize that Jesus is alive and all powerful.

This encounter was also in 2014, but much later in the year. In that moment of time I was spending way too much time meditating on fear and not faith. My faith was being tested.

The enemy tried to sow doubt in my mind. He was whispering lies to me that nothing significant would ever happen in my life. I lied in bed one night, really needing to feel some sort of inner peace, longing for His touch. I really needed one of those special moments with Jesus. I needed to know that God had me in His arms and that l would be ok. I knew the devil was lying to me trying to get my focus off God. That is what the devil tries to do; is to get our focus off God. I needed to have some reassurance, and to once again hear the voice of God. I felt as if I was dry and alone. This was an encounter in my wilderness season.

Wrapped in the Arms of Jesus

Lying on my bed with my eyes closed, listening and worshipping to the song "Oceans" by "Hillsong," Jesus sweeps me away and I see Jesus and Myself standing on the sea of Galilee. There I found myself wrapped in my lovers arms, with waves crashing around our feet, the wind blowing through my hair, standing In total contentment in Indescribable Peace. Jesus says to me, "I Am strengthening your Faith" And just because He can, He takes my hand and gives me a twirl on the water. How I appreciate these special moments and Encounters with the Lord, Jesus My lover of my soul.

Jesus is so amazing. When we think we can't, He reminds us that we can. Just when I needed to feel and hear from Him, He appeared and put me to ease, once again, receiving Peace Beyond understanding.

This chapter is after all about feeling like you are in the wilderness place. I would be the biggest hypocrite if I said that everything in my life and in my mind is all smooth sailing. No, I honestly can't. I too have battles in my mind.

That year in particular was one of the most challenging years for me, not just things I went through, but doubt that crept in, my thoughts had raced away with me. Regular life challenges started in the first week of the new year with my car's window that got smashed and I did not have finances at that time for unplanned expenses. This was a challenge in my mind and emotions. Fear had subtly crept in my mind, and all of a sudden I started fearing about my future. Questions I asked myself would be like; What is happening to my life? Will I ever be successful? Will I ever get married? Will I ever be a mother? Thoughts like; I don't feel fulfilled. This went on for months, there were many nights I cried myself to sleep. I constantly had a knot in my stomach, and I did not have the strength to tell anyone about how I felt. Only I carried these worries and no one else knew. That very Peace and no fear attitude I mentioned wasn't what I was walking in. There I was, feeling all alone in a wilderness season. I didn't realize that I was going through a wilderness time, and going through this time, I completely forgot about the revelation that God had given me about being in the wilderness. I was so desperate for answers. My eyes shifted from Jesus to fear. It happened without me even realizing it.

Eventually one day, having a complete meltdown in my room, crying my heart out, sobbing, I said; "God please, why am I feeling like this?" This meltdown was a couple weeks before I had to preach on the topic "having confidence in Crisis." As you can see, I was having a tough time with that one, in that moment of time I was not even close to having any confidence.

I Heard Him Say

"Your eyes have shifted princess, just by a degree, but it shifted. It shifted from me to your fear and worry. You have to have magnet eyes, your eyes have to connect with mine as a magnet to metal, such a strong attraction that nothing can break that connection. Keep your eyes on my eyes," said the Lord.

I felt such a sense of relief after hearing that, and repented for focusing on the worry instead of the promise. I started once again focusing on the eyes of Jesus and refused to pay attention to the fear. Everyday wasn't easy, but the more I focused on Jesus the more I declared that He knew my future, the more Peace I received and my Joy returned to me. When we are going through a tough time, there is so much power in the life-giving word of God. There is great power in declaring scripture over our life, to think, the very scripture that we declare over our circumstances, is the very breath of God which created the whole world. It is that breath that you are declaring over your life. Job 22:28, "You will declare a thing, And it will be established for you; So light will shine on you always." He wants our eyes to be fixed on Him.

I challenge you, start declaring out loud verses out the Bible that is directed to your circumstance, and see the change, see the power and see the results in that.

The actual wilderness in Israel, is the most beautiful place I have ever seen. Nothing but rocky mountains and the fullness of His Presence. It is my favorite place in the world.

Being in the wilderness is not that bad. If you are there right now, be encouraged, you are there only to come out stronger. God can work with and mold us when we are in that place. I also told you that I had a little secret about being in the wilderness. God showed me principles about the wilderness, and revealed to me the importance of being in such a space at specific times in our lives.

Wilderness

Where intimacy with The King lavishes upon us during extreme reliance and nothing else satisfies but His Spirit.

Where

This is the place where God can work with us. It's the place where we feel like we have nothing but Him. If we come to a point where we have lost everything in life, or just feel completely alone, feel as if nothing is going our way, have that dry feeling I was talking about, feel like you are dead inside, this is the place that God can truly show you what and who He is. If we are in this place in our life, we won't have anything to lose. We don't have anything, or anyone to make a way BUT God. This is the place where God can show you His mighty power.

Intimacy With the King

This wilderness place is a place to be intimate with God. It is the place where the only one you have is God. This is where He overwhelms us with His Love and compassion. This is the place where you experience the gentleness of His heart. You experience the sweet whispers of His voice and the comforting touch of His presence. It is amazing how God created us, He knows that when we are in a desert place that He has a chance with us because it is at that point in our life that we tried all our own ways of working and thinking things out, and trying to sort and fix things by ourselves with no success. When we feel like we have nothing and nothing worked out for us, is the time that God can take over. He allows us to make our own decisions, and we have the free choice to decide to either follow His direction or not. When we mess up, He says, ok my child, now I can work with you and show you exactly what I can do in your life. Intimacy with God becomes a reality when we find ourselves in a wilderness season. We then realize that He IS real, and He IS alive and that we can encounter His love. God takes this opportunity to have me and you ALL to Himself. He takes this opportunity to spend intimate time with His most precious part of creation, He takes delight in spending time with the one He created. You have nothing to lose by giving God a chance to show you how much He loves you. He already showed us His love by sending Jesus to forgive us from our sins and saved us from going to hell, but let Him show you over and over how much He loves you. Embrace this time of getting to know the one who calls you His beloved.

Lavishes

Not only can we have this intimacy with the King, but this very intimacy lavishes during this wilderness time. Do you know what the word lavish means? In the google dictionary it is bestowing someone or something in extravagant quantities, it is to give freely, to spend, to shower, and to pour. It means MORE than enough. So in this wilderness time, our intimacy grows strong with Him. He freely pours Himself out on us more than enough until we overflow. I don't think we always grasp the reality of Him pouring HIMSELF out unto us. Let's think for a minute about who He is. He is Alpha and Omega, the beginning and the end, He is Savior, He is Jehovah, Immanuel, He is strength, He is Love, He is Joy and Peace, He is faithful, He is generous and gracious, He is victory, He is patient and kind, He is powerful yet gentle, He is omnipresent and omnipotent. Our God is full of dimension and full of deepness. He is after all, I Am, He is anything and everything we need. So now I say again, during the wilderness season, God has the opportunity to pour all of himself out over you, through you and in you, now sit back and ponder on who and what is being imparted into you. If He is in you, then simply all of the above and more, is IN you.

During Extreme Reliance

Let's face it, if we find ourselves in the wilderness, we feel as if there is nothing and no one, it is a time of absolute desperation. We cry out, "if something can just go my way, if someone can just help." This is the time we EXTREMELY rely on God realizing that only He can make away.

Nothing Else Satisfies but His Spirit

While and after being in this season of our life, we come to the realization that there is absolutely nothing in the world that can truly satisfy us but the Spirit and Presence of God. It's a connection that no one can explain. His DNA is my DNA, so obviously there must be some sort of longing in our Spirits to be connected with He who created our spirit. A part of Him is in me, so nothing else will satisfy me but the one who created me. He is the one who knows the number of hair on my head, the one who called me before I was in my mother's womb, the one who set me apart and called me He's own. Nothing else can fully satisfy but Him.

This is the place where you are totally alone with God, totally relying on Him and totally desperate for Him. This is where you are separated and can be intimate with God. The physical Wilderness in Israel is the most beautiful place to be at. When you stand in the wilderness in Israel, all you hear is silence, it's the perfect place to be alone and intimate with God. How much more intimate in the spiritual wilderness. When we go through a season in our lives where we feel as if we're in the wilderness, we think it's the worst place to be and we just want to get out. We feel as if we're running dry, as if nothing is going the right way, as if the breakthrough is just not coming. Don't despise the wilderness, embrace the experience. This is not a bad place to be in at all. Just because it feels as if God is distant and not answering prayers doesn't mean that He is distant. He hasn't gone anywhere. He is working behind the scenes. There are specific things that God does in the wilderness. This is the place where God strengthens you, equips you, rejuvenates you, embraces you and loves on you. Think of it this way, picture yourself getting ready for a boxing match for the world title. You've gone to a deserted island, just you and your trainer. The training is intense but when you come off that island you will be well equipped, strengthened and ready for the match. That is the wilderness; it is your time of training, where it is just you and God, He is busy strengthening you. The wilderness season is the time where God can reveal things to you. He reveals those special secrets and hidden treasures.

Sometimes the only way that God gets a chance to be with you and have a moment with you, is when you find yourself in the wilderness. I tell you what, the moment you become content in your wilderness season, is the moment the devil flees for his life. The thing is; the devil THINKS that when you are in your dry season when you think there is no more reason for life that this is the time that he has won. He THINKS that that is the knockout of the match. But when you are content and peaceful in the wilderness, he gets frightened and shakes with fear. When you step out of the wilderness, when you step out of your training season, you step out rejuvenated, refreshed with the living waters that you got directly from the King Himself, you will be strengthened and ready to walk uprightly in victory. When you get up and step out, the devil gets the shock of his life, his eyes widened with fear and he says to himself, "ooooooh nooooo!" the child of God is UP.

Encounter Prayer

Pray this out loud with me:

Lord Jesus, I know this is for my good. I know you are working on my behalf. Help me to see the beauty in this season.

Lisa Fowler

Encounter Notes

God Encounters

Encounter Notes

Lisa Fowler

Encounter Notes

5

The Power of the Free

John 8:36: "Therefore if the Son makes you free, you shall be free indeed"

This is, again, one of my favorite verses in the Bible. What in life, is greater than freedom? What is greater than the freedom that Jesus Christ has given us? I know some of you are asking, but what exactly have we been set free of? Do you carry guilt and shame? What about anger, resentment or rejection? What about the lies that the enemy tells us or those times we read the Bible and have no clue what we are reading. We have been set free from bondage, sin and shame.

My dear friend, if Jesus said that He set you free, then that is exactly what He did. When Jesus was crucified on that cross a couple thousand years ago, He said three life changing words, "It is done." This means, anything and everything that you need, He has done it. If you need any type of deliverance from an addiction, Jesus already did it for you, He already set you free from it. It is up to you and me to make the choice to accept and live by it. The Son has set you free and you shall be free indeed.

I am so grateful that Jesus has set me free from: any type of bondage, free from the lies of the enemy, those lies can be loud from time to time. If you are hearing anything that does not line up with the Word of God, please know that, that is a lie and that satan is trying to get you down. If we just realize the power that lies in our freedom. There's a deeper level of power to tap into - once we realise the depth of our freedom. Can you imagine what type of Victory we can live in, when we come to that place in our lives, that as soon as we hear a lie, we recognise immediately that it is a lie, and then immediately rebuke it, No devil in hell can get us down and stop us from fulfilling the purpose that God has for us.

Expressing our Freedom

2 Samuel 6:22 "and I will be even more undignified than this"

It's an incredible feeling to know you've been set free—and even more powerful to declare, "I am free." Thank you, Jesus, for breaking the chains that once held me back and weighed me down. But here's the truth: too often, we stop at just saying we're free, without actually stepping into that freedom. We talk the talk, but where's the walk? People don't just want to hear about freedom—they want to see it lived out.

We have to start living out our freedom. Picture this for a moment. Someone standing in church declaring during a praise song about the freedom of the Lord, but they have no smile on their face, and are not even clapping their hands. How can we say something and our actions don't line up with our words? If we are declaring through a praise song that we are free and singing about having Joy or gratitude for Jesus, then our expression should line up with the words that are coming out of your mouth. Now picture someone, during a praise song, with at least a smile on their face, clapping their hands, and let's push it a little to even a little side to side movement. Can you see the difference?

We need to start expressing our freedom, it's time that we start showing the world that the enemy is under our feet. We need to live like we are the head and not the tail. Our actions express our belief in our freedom.

Four Elements of Being Free.

1. **Fearless:** Knowing we are truly free empowers us to live without fear.

   Psalm 27:3, "Though an army may encamp against me, My heart shall not fear, though war may rise against me, in this I will be confident"

We can walk around like a fearless lion, and not have a worry in the world. We walk around knowing and declaring that: this is who I am in Christ, that I have victory and power

Lisa Fowler

in the name of Jesus, that Jesus lives in me and I in Him. Knowing that we are free, makes us fearless and bold enough in any situation to proclaim the name of Jesus. We want to proclaim everything there is about Jesus. We want to proclaim that nothing and no one can come against the name of Jesus.

There are some amazing synonyms in the google dictionary for the word "fearless." Words like, courageous, confident and dynamic. We need to be confident in who we are and in what we believe.

True confidence and courage begin when we fully understand our freedom.

Some of the synonyms for the word dynamic. Potent, positive, bold and effective. When we start to function in our freedom, we step into a place where we can be potent and effective for the Kingdom of God.

Now there once was a king who showed us how to be free in the Lord, to be confident in God, and that was King David – I call Him fearless David

> *2 SAMUEL 6:14 "Then David danced before the Lord with all His might,"*

David is a prime example of being free in God's presence. David was bold enough to express his freedom in front of anyone. He wasn't afraid of who was looking at him or what the people said about him. He was confident in God. He danced with all his might in the presence of God, even ripping his clothes, becoming humble and vulnerable, totally transparent.

2 Samuel 6: 20-22 "20 Then David returned to bless his household and Michal the daughter of Saul came out to meet David and said, How glorious was the king of Israel today, uncovering himself today in the eyes of the maids of his servants as one of the base fellows shamelessly uncovers himself. So David said to Michal, It was before the Lord, who chose me instead of your father and all his house to appoint me ruler over the people of the Lord, over Israel. Therefore I will play music before the Lord. And I will be even more undignified than this and will be humble in my own sight."

I love that David says, "And I will be even more undignified than this." It doesn't matter how weird we look while praising God, it doesn't matter if we have two left feet or two right feet, if our arms look funny or we jump up and down. We are humbling ourselves, using your body as a living sacrifice and giving all of who we are to the one who created us.

Once I had a vision of what was going on in the Spirit while someone was dancing while praising God. I saw the enemy throwing hand grenades at the person dancing, but nothing was touching them as they danced and expressed their freedom, the devil missed with every throw. As they moved from side to side he kept on missing. Nothing can touch us if we keep on moving, and this is exactly what David was doing in the Spirit with a natural movement, he was dodging hand grenades left right and centre.

Let's become fearless.

2.   **Relentless:** Freedom fuels a relentless drive—once you understand it, there's no holding back.

I love to give the meaning of words, it helps break it down and really get the truth behind a word. The meaning of relentless in the google dictionary is persistent, constant, uninterrupted and unstoppable. Here is a phrase for you. If you abandon every distraction and be uninterrupted in His Presence you will become unstoppable for Jesus. Be relentless for God, be consistent, be persistent, seek Him with everything in you, and no weapon formed against you will stop you from doing what God has called you to do.

Unfortunately in life though, when we don't get our way, or when the breakthrough is taking too long, we become STAGNANT instead of PERSISTENT.

We become still, motionless, immobile, lifeless, dead and lazy, we don't feel like praising, we don't feel like walking in our calling, it becomes too heavy, too difficult, we remain on the sofa instead of standing up and showing the devil that He who is in me is greater than he who is in the world. He that is in me is greater than he who is in my situation, instead of standing up and saying, I'm going to show the devil that I will praise and rejoice for my God is the great and greatly to be praised. He is the great I am, the beginning the end, my healer my savior and redeemer.

> *Luke 1:39-41 "Now Mary arose in those days and went into the hill country with haste to the city of Judah and entered the house of Zacharias and greeted Elizabeth. And it happened when Elizabeth heard the greeting of Mary, that the babe leaped in her womb and Elizabeth was filled with the Holy Spirit."*

Now for those who might not know, at that current time, Mary was pregnant with Jesus and Elizabeth pregnant with John the baptized. As Mary greeted Elizabeth, John had an encounter with Jesus. John had his first encounter with the Holy Spirit while in the womb of his mother.

> *2 Corinthians 3:17, "Now the Lord is the Spirit, and where the Spirit of the Lord is, there is freedom."*

I get excited reading that scripture. Where the Spirit of the Lord is, there is freedom. If you have accepted Jesus as your Lord and Savior, that means He lives in you, and so does His Spirit, which means freedom is living in the inside of you. Jesus set us free a long time ago, we just have to choose to accept it.

Lisa Fowler

When John encountered the Presence of Jesus while in his mother's womb, something powerful happened—he was touched by the Holy Spirit. And with that encounter came a taste of true freedom, the kind that breaks chains and awakens purpose. Even in the womb, John couldn't remain still; that baby leaped with joy at the nearness of his Savior. He wasn't just reacting—he was responding to divine freedom. From that moment on, John was marked. That encounter was transformational. It set the course for an extraordinary life, one fueled by purpose, boldness, and passion. John was relentless for Jesus, unwavering in his mission, unshaken by opposition. His life became a living echo of the freedom he first felt in the presence of Christ.

One moment encountering God while John was in his mothers womb changed his life. The Bible says that John lived in the wilderness, eating locusts and honey, he was a voice in the wilderness shouting out, prepare the way of the Lord. He didn't care who heard him, he was free for he knew the son had set him free. Before John was even born, he did a little side to side.

Let's become unstoppable and relentless for God.

3. **Expectant:** When we truly understand our freedom, we won't settle - we begin to live with a constant expectation of the more of God.

When we truly understand our freedom in Christ, everything changes. We stop settling for a life of limitation, complacency. Instead, we begin to live with a deep and constant expectation for the more of God. The greater works He wants to do through us. Jesus Himself declared in John 14:12, "Most assuredly, I say to you, he who believes in Me, the works that I do he will do also; and greater works than these he will do, because I go to My Father." That isn't just a nice verse to memorize, it's a promise we're called to walk in. I would love to step into a season where John 14:12 becomes a daily walk and not just something I'm praying about.

How often do we actually expect that to be our reality? We need to wake up each day with a holy anticipation, ready to partner with God. Our posture should be one of expectation, openness and readiness, saying, "OK God, what do You have planned for today? What are You up to today? and how can I be a part of the plan? Use me, Lord, I'm willing. I'm available. I'm expecting John 14:12 to come to life in me."

Freedom isn't just a status, it's an invitation. An invitation to live boldly, to dream bigger, to believe for miracles, and to expect God to move through us in ways beyond what we could ever imagine.

Let's become expectant for the more of God.

4. **Excited:** Knowing we are free unlocks a joy and excitement like no other.

We need to get back to the place where we are overwhelmed with excitement about who God is. We need to get excited about how great He is, and get excited about how powerful, majestic and miraculous He is. Psalms 30:5, "Weeping may endure for a night, but joy comes in the morning." Wake up with excitement and see the enemy frightened. Wake up with excitement and get ready for your assignment.

> *Acts 16.25-26. (AMP) "But about midnight, as Paul and Silas were praying and singing hymns of praise to God, and the [other] prisoners were listening to them, Suddenly there was a great earthquake, so that the very foundations of the prison were shaken; and at once all the doors were opened and everyone's shackles were unfastened."*

Even though Paul and Silas were in a physical state of captivity they knew that their Spirits were free, there was just a freedom within the depth of their belly that when they functioned in their freedom the very thing that was holding them back was shaken to pieces, not only were their chains broken, but those shackles were loosened.

Not only does Jesus break our chains, but He loosens shackles usually when we hear a sermon and watch a video of someone breaking free from chains, we see the person with their hands free but they still have the shackles around their wrist. This is not spoken of when most people preach the message of "Broken chains." Those shackles resemble shame, death, depression, anxiety, worry And bondage.

Acts 16 in the AMP says that everyone's shackles were UNFASTENED.

This is what Jesus did for us, he paid the price for our full freedom, not just broken chains and shackles on wrists. Jesus set us completely free, He didn't leave any shackles on our wrists. Whens Jesus set us free, He didn't leave any residue of bondage, He took it all. If the Son has set you free, you are free indeed.

> *REV 1:18, "I am He that liveth and was dead and behold I am alive forevermore amen and have the keys of hell and of Death"*

Jesus did not go to hell and back to get a hammer to smash the chains, He went and got the KEY and UNFASTENED your shackles. He has completely unfastened you from any reminder of shame, he has taken away the fear and anxiety of our past.

Lets get excited about our freedom!

Lisa Fowler

Remember, the Four Elements of being Free are:

Fearless
Relentless
Expectant
Excited

Encounter Prayer

Pray this out loud with me:

Jesus, thank you for setting me free. Thank you for not only breaking my chains but loosening me from anxiety about my past. Help me express my gratitude. Help me to be fearless and bold to proclaim your name.

Encounter Notes

_____

_____

_____

_____

_____

_____

_____

_____

Encounter Notes

Lisa Fowler

Encounter Notes

6

How To Encounter God

His Fragrance

I remember the first time I had an encounter with the fragrance of Jesus. It happened at an archaeological site in Galilee, Israel. One of the only synagogues they've found where Jesus could have been in. There were only two synagogues found in that area and we know that Jesus spent a lot of time in Galilee. We were touring the site. I decided to step away for a few minutes as I was feeling a little overwhelmed with all the people around me and wanted to take in the moment of where I was actually standing. I felt like I needed a few minutes alone to pray and worship. I felt a draw from the Lord to get away, to separate myself. I put my head on the stones of the ancient synagogue and immediately I smelt the most beautiful fragrance I've ever smelt. It was a sweet fragrance but not too sweet. It smelt like a mixture of different types of anointing oils and a dab of perfume. If someone saw me I'm sure they thought, "what is that person doing smelling the stones?" But I couldn't get enough of that smell. I looked up to see if anyone was around me, thinking that maybe someone with strong perfume was standing behind me. No one was there. I asked The Lord what I was smelling and He said, "You're smelling my fragrance." My only thought was, WOW. I put my face back on the stones and hugged the wall. I just stayed there while the group of women toured the rest of the place and then went shopping. I knew that I couldn't rush that moment. I knew that God set that moment aside for me to encounter His fragrance. My greatest desire is to experience ALL of who He is and when he creates a moment in time for me to experience Him, I'm going to take it. I enjoyed the sweet presence of the Lord for the rest of the time that we were at that site.

Sometimes we need to step away. Step away from what we are doing. Step away from the noise. Step away from the hustle and bustle. Step away and separate ourselves from what is going on around us. I hear the Lord say, *"come away, come away with me, let me show you what I see. Let me encounter you."* In order for me to have received that encounter I had to step away from the group. At that moment I wasn't supposed to be doing what the others were doing. God had a different plan for me and I had to be obedient to it. Maybe it's time for you to step away from what other people are doing and saying, for you to have the opportunity to receive what God has for you. I had to get quiet. God was already waiting for me. If I didn't step away I would have missed my moment with Him. He planned that encounter for me but I had to make the time to spend with him. We need to be obedient in the moment of the draw. As soon as you feel God drawing you close, take it. Take every chance you get to be with him. I don't want to miss one thing he has for me. When he says stop, you stop. When he says come, you come.

We need to learn to get quiet in God's Presence. How do we hear another person speak if we are talking all the time? Once we pray and worship and then get quiet, God can have the opportunity to speak, then He can have the opportunity to encounter us.

A Vision of the Nations

In this vision I was swept up to a mountain top again. It started very similar to a vision I had before. If you can, picture the highest part of the wilderness in Israel. It's a beautiful array of light brown almost golden desert made of rocky Mountains. In the vision I saw Jesus and I together. Both of us were dressed in white and we were dancing together on the mountain top. When the dance ended I walked toward and stood at the edge of the mountain. Not able to see anything but grey clouds. I then saw Jesus standing behind me. He wrapped me in a Tallit (a Hebrew prayer Shawl) and he held me tight. He kept standing behind me for a while. I felt so much comfort and peace. I saw His arms around me. I saw His face against mine and I saw His brown hair flowing in the wind. Then I saw Jesus stretch out his hand and sweep away the clouds. I looked down and saw all the nations of the world. It looked like I was looking at earth from space. I saw the ocean and the nations from America to Australia and everything in between. I saw the whole of Africa, Europe and Asia. I asked Jesus why He was showing me this. I thought it looked amazing but I didn't understand why He was showing me "what looked like earth." Jesus answered and said, "Princess, I'm going to take you to the nations." I came out of the vision and was blown away. I always wanted to travel to the nations but I'd never asked God about it before I had the vision. God knows our deepest desires.

What was I doing before I had this vision?

I was laying on my bed, praying In the spirit and worshiping. I was thanking Him for His goodness.

Thanksgiving is the Key

Psalm 100:4 Enter His gates with thanksgiving, and His courts with praise; give thanks to Him and praise his name.

Colossians 4:2 Continue earnestly in prayer, being vigilant in it with thanksgiving

Psalms 50:14 Offer to God thanksgiving, and pay your vows to the most high.

Psalm 147:7 Sing to the Lord with thanksgiving; Sing praises on the harp to our God.

Psalm 69:30 I will praise the name of God with a song, and will magnify Him with thanksgiving

Psalm 26:7 That I may proclaim with the voice of thanksgiving, and tell of all your wondrous works

Thanksgiving and praying in tongues are the keys to opening the portals to the supernatural. God loves the fragrance of praise and thanksgiving. "His gates are open for those who enter with thanksgiving and his courts are open to those who praise." Colossians 4:2 encourages us to always have thanksgiving in our heart while we pray. Continue earnestly in prayer. Earnestly in the Merriam-Webster dictionary means; in an earnest and serious manner: not lightly, casually or flippantly. We are not to take prayer and thanksgiving lightly. Our thanksgiving and praise is like a sweet aroma unto God. He loves to encounter us while we worship Him. He loves to reveal Himself to us while we pray and worship. There is no limit to what God can do and show us, especially while we worship Him.

The Glory Cloud

I was laying on my bed one day while I was in Israel, exhausted. There was a season that I served in a guest house in Jerusalem, I lived there for months at a time. It was hard work and long hours, serving people all day. If I wasn't serving I was cleaning and if I wasn't cleaning I was cooking and if I wasn't cooking I was touring people around the streets of Jerusalem. Walking the streets of Jerusalem was my favorite. But as I laid on my bed I prayed a simple prayer. "God you'll need to pick me up because I'm just too tired to get up." Suddenly I had a vision and I saw myself standing at the bottom of one of the staircases in Jerusalem. I saw Jesus on top hidden in a cloud and all I could see was His hand reaching out from the cloud. His hand came down and He took me by my hand and pulled me up into the cloud. It was as if I flew up to Him. He took me Inside the cloud. I couldn't see anything but a white bright light. All I saw was the bright white light with what seemed like lighting bolts and electrical currents flowing through it. I couldn't see Jesus but I heard Him say, "welcome to my glory cloud." He said, "you have access to this Glory cloud, you have access whenever you need me."

The vision ended and I immediately jumped up and knelt down at the side of my bed. I felt the fear of the Lord all over me. I stayed on my knees for a while just in awe of God's Glory. I was so thankful that Jesus made me feel worthy to see His Glory cloud. I wasn't tired anymore. I felt refreshed and ready to go.

He Is a God That Comforts

My grandma was my whole life, she was my best friend, she was the one I told everything to. She was the kind of grandma that every child deserves. When she went to be with the Lord it broke me. I felt like my heart could not heal. My best friend was gone forever. I was sad and depressed for months after she passed. I could not get over it, I was so desperate to have one more hug, I just wanted to tell her how much I loved her, just one more time. I was going through a very difficult time of grief. I needed to be comforted and nothing and no one could give me that comfort. One night I went to bed and while I was laying there I sobbed and cried out to the Lord. "God please comfort me, I can't do this anymore. Nothing and no one can help me. Nothing can make me feel better. My heart is broken, I feel like I can't breath. I miss grandma so much and I will never see her again." I closed my eyes and opened them again. To my surprise, I saw 3 angels sitting on my bed. At first I felt a little frightened. I didn't know what I was looking at. I blinked a few times and wiped my eyes. I then saw it, as if my eyes were opened. There were 2 Angels sitting on the end of my bed and one Angel beside me on my left. I said, "God, what is happening, why are they here"? I heard the Lord say, I have sent my ministering Angels to you, they will stay with you and comfort you. Those Angels sat with me all night. I felt so much peace. I had the best sleep I've had in almost a year.

God's heart hurts when His children are hurting. He desires to comfort us. Are you open to His comfort?

2 Corinthians 1:3 Blessed be the God and Father of our Lord Jesus Christ, the Father of mercies and God of all comfort.

Isaiah 41:10 Fear not, for I am with you; Be not dismayed, for I am your God. I will strengthen you, Yes, I will help you, I will uphold you with my righteous right hand.

Psalm 94:19 In the multitude of my anxieties within me, Your comforts delight my soul.

John 14:27 Peace I leave with you, My peace I give to you; not as the world gives do I give to you. Let not your heart be troubled, neither let it be afraid.

Matthew 11:28 Come to me, all who labor and are heavy laden, and I will give you rest.

Psalm 34:18 The Lord is near to those who have a broken heart, And saves such as have a contrite spirit.

I love this faith filled Journey. Just recently I was encouraging a friend who was worried about her future. I know it's hard to hear at the moment but God has you in the palm of His hands. The greatest thing about this journey is that if you have given your life to Jesus and you have totally surrendered to Him, there is no way that He will fail you. He's got your back, He will work all things out for those who love Him. Romans 8:28

I remember a time when I was stressed about my future. I have mentioned this before, I was stressed at the thought of not getting married one day. All I ever wanted was to be a wife and a mom. But God knew what He was doing. He had all things planned. He knew every step before I was born. He knew that I would get married to the most amazing man in the world.

Another dove encounter brought me and my amazing husband together. I was praying for confirmation that this was the time for Joshua and I to get married. I asked God this time not to see a white dove but for someone to talk to me about a white dove in the next 24 hours. 10 minutes later Joshua texted me and said, "the next time I see you, remind me to tell you about something." So I said, "just tell me now." He said, "While preaching in Brazil one night everyone started gasping and looked amazed, I looked up and there was a white dove sitting on a banister above me." The people were amazed because that kind of bird was not indigenous to that region. The white dove stayed above him until he walked off the platform. As he walked off, the dove flew off.

I was blown away when I was done reading his text. I went into a cold sweat. I was nervous and excited all in one. Not only did God confirm exactly What I was praying about but he confirmed it through the very person I was praying about marrying!

After Jesus, Joshua is the best thing that has happened to me. We are happily married and we get to share encounters together.

Lisa Fowler

How Do We Encounter Him?

We need to spend time with Him, we need to meditate. When you go to bed at night, before you fall asleep say, "speak Lord for I am listening." We need to quiet down. After saying "speak Lord, I am Listening," then that is what you do, just listen, no more words, no more requests. Just be quiet and listen.

> *Gen 28:10-15 "Now Jacob went out from Beersheba and went toward Haran. So he came to a certain place and stayed there all night, because the sun had set. And he took one of the stones from that place and put it at his head, and he lay down in that place to sleep. Then he dreamed, and behold, a ladder was set up on the earth, and its top reached to heaven; and there the angels of God were ascending and descending on it. And behold, the Lord stood above it and said: "I am the Lord God of Abraham your father and the God of Isaac; the land on which you lie I will give to you and your descendants. Also your descendants shall be as the dust of the earth; you shall spread abroad to the west and the east, to the north and the south; and in you and in your seed all the families of the earth shall be blessed. Behold, I am with you and will keep you wherever you go, and will bring you back to this land; for I will not leave you until I have done what I have spoken to you."*

Who is the rock? Jesus is the rock, firm, unshakable, and eternal. He is our foundation, our refuge, our steady place in a world that constantly shifts. When we choose to lay our head down on Jesus, we're not just resting, we're surrendering. We're saying, "I trust you." I give you full access to my heart, my mind, and my spirit." It's in that place of surrender that he begins to do what he does best: speak, reveal, restore, and lead.

When we rest on the rock, we make space for heaven to meet earth. We invite divine encounters, dreams, and visions that can only come from being close to His heart. Laying your head on the rock opens up heavenly portals of glory where you don't just hear about God's presence, but you experience it. It all starts with resting on the rock. Encounters happen where intimacy begins.

Have You Heard of Heaven's Sound Room?

In a dream one night (after saying, "speak Lord, I am listening") I found myself walking down a long bright white hallway. The only thing I could see was a white bright light and white walls. I couldn't see any doors but only one door at the end of the hallway. When I came close to the door, the door opened. I stepped inside the room and saw black music notes flying around the room. I could grab them and hold them in my hands. I saw all types of instruments, sound waves in different colors and things that looked like sound boards. In my dream I said, "God, where am I?" He immediately replied and said, "welcome to the sound room of heaven" here you have access to every sound possible. Grab notes and make your own melody to me."

Job 33:15 NKJV In a dream, in a vision of the night, when deep sleep falls upon men, while slumbering on their beds, then He opens the ears of men, and seals their instruction.

I remember waking up the next morning with excitement in my heart. I couldn't believe that I was allowed to see a sound room in Heaven. Not only does God sing over us, (Zephaniah 3:17, "The Lord your God in your midst, The Mighty One, will save; He will rejoice over you with gladness, He will quiet you with His love, He will rejoice over you with singing.") But He loves the sound of your voice, He loves the sound of your worship, He loves when you make a sweet melody unto Him. Your worship is like a sweet fragrance unto God.

Field Of Glory Vision

My husband and I were planning to have a tent revival on our land in Texas.

As I walked the property praying, I heard intense worship and heard angels ascending and descending but I couldn't see them! I didn't see them but I heard them. I asked God, "God where are they"? "Look" said the Lord. As I focused I saw what seemed to be a dramatic musical happening in front of my eyes. Angels ascending and descending on all four corners of our property, worshipping intensely, as I prayed in the spirit I saw more of the musical unfold. Angels sending beams of fire from one corner to another, enclosing our land with a fiery fence. As I watched and heard this dramatic intense angelic scene, I saw them shooting the beams of fire into the heavens and as the beams from all four corners touched In the heavens, there was an explosion. Down came flames of fire and each flame had a miracle written in it. Each flame had a word written in it. Healing, finances, breakthrough, Hearing, sight, limbs, hearts, kidneys etc. These flames of miracles landed on the grass and started setting the land on fire! Holy Fire! Glory Fire! Presence Fire! I heard the Lord say, "I have prepared the ground for the ground you are about to step on is Holy ground, this ground is drenched in miracles, I have already sent them down from Heaven, come and get it says the Lord."

Encounter Prayer

Pray this out loud with me:

Lord, may encountering you become normal to me. May God encounters become real to me. Jesus I lay my head down on you and I am open for you to show me things I have not seen.

Lisa Fowler

Encounter Notes

God Encounters

Encounter Notes

Lisa Fowler

Encounter Notes

7

Joy is God's Medicine

Proverbs 17:22 ESV "A joyful heart is good medicine, but a crushed spirit dries up the bones."

I heard a gentle whisper, "Why use someone else's testimony if you can use your own?"

It was a sunny Saturday morning in Texas. We enjoyed an early game of pickleball, had a great lunch and went on with our day, not knowing that our lives would radically change over night. Have you ever had the feeling of a rug being pulled out from under your feet? I had never experienced that feeling before May 25, 2024. You know when your life takes a sudden and unexpected turn. A month later my husband and I were driving down the road, still trying to comprehend what had happened. I told Joshua, "you know baby, we were on a certain path knowing where we were going, we had a plan and a vision for our future and we were working hard towards it and in a matter of seconds we were not heading that direction anymore." Instead we were crying out to God to save our lives. We screamed as loud as we could, "Jesus save us, Jesus please save our family!" The amount of fear that gripped us is impossible to explain, I'm talking bone chilling, breathtaking, staring death in the face kind of fear.

I put the kids to bed and went to bed myself. Then at 10:42pm my husband heard what sounded like a woman screaming, he immediately felt that something was wrong. He felt a nudge from the Holy Spirit to get me and the kids. He came running in the bedroom and he shouted, "baby, wake up, I'll get Selah (our then 3 year old daughter) and you get Judah (our then 1 year old son) and meet me in the bathroom under the stairs. I had no idea what was happening but I jumped out of bed, ran to the nursery and grabbed my baby boy. As I ran out of the room I heard windows shattering. I met Joshua in the bathroom and as soon as I closed the door the nightmare began.

There we were, standing in a place I had never in my life imagined being in. Hiding under our staircase in a tiny bathroom. Joshua holding Selah and me holding Judah, Selah shaking violently in her daddy's arms. Judah holding me tight with his face burrowed in my neck crying and shaking. We were smack center, in the middle of the most hellacious wind. It sounded like a demonic scream and a whistling sound of a train. We felt heat and moisture rising up to our knees. I remember smelling the earth and feeling like the house was about to get sucked up. A F3 tornado ripped through our house while we were in it. No sirens, no alarms, no warning, only a nudge from the Holy Spirit to get

God Encounters

his family. Our house was a direct hit. That monster of a storm was relentless, it destroyed everything in its path. In the midst of a thousand thoughts, I remember thinking, this is it, we are dying tonight. We were either going to get sucked up in the air or something was going to crush us. All we could do in that moment was violently pray in tongues and scream, "Jesus save us, save our family." It felt as if we were stuck in time, it felt like we were in the tornado for an eternity. We could hear things crashing into our house and didn't know what was going to happen next. The worst thunder, lightning and wind I've ever heard. While crying out to God to save us, Joshua heard the Lord say, "command the wind." He immediately started screaming, "leave this land, leave this land." I started to shout it out loud with him and by the third time of commanding the wind it was as if the storm exhaled and it lifted. It felt as if we were characters in the movie Twister, but it wasn't a movie and we were not characters, it was reality. Joshua left the bathroom to see what had happened. He came back and said, "baby, you don't want to see this." I stepped out to see devastation everywhere, our house was destroyed.

Electric wires all around, 12 - 50ft steel beams pierced through our house like torpedos. There was devastation all around. My parents, brother and his family were in the guest house on our land. My dad watched the tornado hit our house knowing that we were in the house but not knowing if we were alive. We walked out of the house without one scratch on our bodies. It was a total miracle that we survived that night. If we hadn't called on the name of Jesus, we would have been dead. If we didn't know God, we would have been dead. If Joshua didn't encounter God's voice, we would have been dead. If Joshua wasn't home that night, me and the kids would have been dead.

Sixteen weeks later battling with major trauma and feeling displaced. By then we had stayed in numerous hotel rooms and a few Airbnb's. Joshua sat on a porch at a condo on the beach in Panama City Beach, FL. He had no words to pray but all he could do was sing, "Jesus you, you restore my soul, you restore my soul" he sang that over and over and in the midst of singing that song he felt God restore him. He received full healing and restoration from the trauma.

It took me a little longer to receive my breakthrough. A week after Joshua received his breakthrough I sat in the living room and I realized that my husband could not give me my breakthrough. Only one person could heal me and that was God. I cried out to Him. "God, I'm so happy for Joshua but I need my breakthrough too, I have no Joy. I feel depressed. I'm smiling and laughing with my kids, but I'm broken on the inside. I don't want to do anything. We experienced and lived through a tornado but my home is gone, there is no going back." I knew I had to be strong for my kids but I was a total mess on the inside. My heart felt like a dried out prune. I had no other words to pray or any song to sing. I'm crying thinking about it. God reminded me of this scripture, Proverbs 17:22 in the ESV *"A joyful heart is good medicine, but a crushed spirit dries up the bones."*

The next day we headed to a conference we were hosting in South Carolina. The day we arrived I prayed and said, "God, I need your medicine. I don't want to live my life feeling dry, I don't want dry bones, I need your Joy." One of my good friends was leading worship at the conference and we laughed all weekend long. Some time on Saturday afternoon, while laughing, I realized that I wasn't fake laughing. I was bubbling from the inside, I had so much Joy spending time with Sarah and spending time in God's presence, It felt like water to my soul. I felt refreshed. I realized that God gave me exactly what I asked for, He gave me His medicine. I had never felt a scripture come to life like Proverbs 17:22 did that day. His Joy became my medicine. I had an encounter with God's Joy, I encountered His medicine. Suddenly I felt watered, I didn't feel dry anymore. Joy was dripping all over me. This was a whole weekend of God's Joy, a whole weekend of God's medicine where the Lord totally healed me. I received my breakthrough and I went back home a new person.

Proverbs 31:25 (The Passion Translation) Bold power and glorious majesty are wrapped around her as she laughs with joy over the latter days.

This has become my go to scripture. I shall laugh without fear because I am wrapped in His bold power and majesty. Trauma does not need to have a hold on you. Fear doesn't need to have a grip on you. I was gripped with fear after the tornado hit us. Bone chilling fear. I remember sitting beside my husband in a hotel room weeks after the storm watching the news. Bad weather was on the way and as soon as I heard the first thunder and lightning strike my body started shaking uncontrollably. Now, I say no to fear, do you? God has set me free through His JOY. Just like the words of that song, "Fear is not my future" by Brandon Lake. Depression is not your future. Trauma is not your future. JOY is! Now say this with me, trauma is not my future, JOY is. Will you join me and say NO to trauma?

Our children, Selah and Judah who practically woke up every night screaming from the trauma of the tornado and slept on Joshua and my chest every night for 17 weeks received their breakthrough after Joshua and I received our peace and joy back. They too began sleeping through the night and started to sleep in their own beds. Just like the oil runs from Aron's beard, so did the oil of breakthrough drip from us onto our kids.

The Best is Yet to Come!

At the time of writing the conclusion of this book, it has now been almost a year since we lost our home and everything in the Tornado. I'm happy to report that we just moved into our new home in Florida. Selah and Judah are sleeping through the night in their own rooms in their own beds. We have begun to see the restoration and even acceleration of the plans of the Lord in our lives. The Lord is opening doors and releasing favor in our lives in an unprecedented manner. I don't share this to boast, but to testify of how these God Encounters have truly changed our lives. So no matter where you are in life, as you read this book, fix your eyes on Jesus. Go after Him with all of your heart. Don't settle for the status quo. Refuse to be satisfied with boring, mundane Sunday morning religiosity. It's not religion, it's a relationship. Pursue His Presence without reservation. Desire His Greater Glory more than your next breath. As you do this, get ready for Jesus to meet with you in your dreams. Get ready for the Lord to dance with you in your visions. Get ready to hear His voice when you pray. Get ready for His Word to come alive as you read it. God Encounters are awaiting you. God is waiting for you. I declare and decree Close encounters of the God-Kind are overtaking you and your family in Jesus name.

Encounter Decree

Decree this Aloud with me:

I Declare and I Decree I am open and ready for God Encounters in Jesus name. My life will never be the same. I will go from Glory to Glory, Strength to Strength, Faith to Faith and from Encounters to Encounters in the Presence of the Lord. God Encounters are my portion. I will lead others into God Encounters and their lives will be forever changed in Jesus name. Amen

Lisa Fowler

Encounter Notes

God Encounters

Encounter Notes

Lisa Fowler

Encounter Notes

Order Your T-Shirts, Books, Awake Coffee & More Today!

Get Your iProphesy Gear & More Today!

AwakeTheWorld.org

Contact Information:

Awake The World, Inc.
PO Box 1833
Lynn Haven, Florida 32444
booking@AwakeTheWorld.org
407-760-8400

For more information regarding distribution, contact
info@advbooks.com

Advantage
BOOKS

Orlando, Florida, USA
"we bring dreams to life"™
www.advbookstore.com

Printed in Dunstable, United Kingdom